Candle in the Wind

Gary Brady

EP BOOKS
1st Floor Venture House, 6 Silver Court, Watchmead,
Welwyn Garden City, UK, AL7 1TS

www.epbooks.org
sales@epbooks.org

EP BOOKS are distributed in the USA by:
JPL Fulfillment
3741 Linden Avenue Southeast,
Grand Rapids, MI 49548.
E-mail: sales@jplfulfillment.com
Tel: 877.683.6935

© Evangelical Press 2014. All rights reserved. No part of this publication may be reproduced, stored in a retrieval system or transmitted, in any form, or by any means, electronic, mechanical, photocopying, recording or otherwise, without the prior permission of the publishers.

First published 2014

British Library Cataloguing in Publication Data available

ISBN 978-1-78397-042-1

Unless otherwise indicated, Scripture quotations are from **The Holy Bible, English Standard Version** (**ESV**), published by HarperCollins Publishers © 2001 by Crossway Bibles, a division of Good News Publishers. Used by permission. All rights reserved.

Printed and bound in the UK by 4edge Limited

To Robert and Sarah

Fellow workers and good friends in Christ

Contents

    Preface 7
    Introduction 11
1. Shaking the tree 15
2. What are Conscience? 27
3. Candle in the Wind 41
4. Thundering beginnings 57
5. Peace perfect peace 73
6. The Paradise of delight 85
7. Seared with a hot iron 103
8. Fully persuaded 121
9. Serve one another in love 139
10. Gimme a penny 155
11. Jesus is Lord 171
12. And the books were opened 191
    Appendix 1 205
    Appendix 2 211
    Appendix 3 215
    A Select Bibliography 241

Preface

The subject of conscience is one that I have been studying for more than half a life time. I believe it was reading a hardback edition of Ole Hallesby's work on the subject as a young man that sparked my initial interest. It was the paradoxical paucity of material on the subject and the abundance of references to conscience elsewhere that served to further spike a desire in me to learn more.

Over the years I have been gathering material on the subject from various sources. Very little of the fruit of these studies has seen the light of day, although in 1995 and 1996 two articles did appear in *Foundations* the journal of the old BEC (now Affinity). I also spoke on the subject on some few occasions to the church here in Childs Hill and once or twice to fellow pastors.

In 2006 I completed a thesis, *A Study of Ideas of the Conscience in Puritan Writings, 1590–1640* as part of the requirements to successfully complete a ThM degree at the John Owen Centre, here in London, in conjunction with Westminster Theological Seminary, Philadelphia.

I have taken the liberty of making extensive use of these two self-penned sources for this present work.

The half buried desire to pull the material together and produce a popular book finally rose to the surface in the summer of 2012 when I came across the excellent book on the subject by Christopher Ash, *Pure Joy*. Initially I thought there was now no need for me to publish anything, given its excellence. Having read it carefully, however, I think that there are some things to add and so I have pursued publication. It seems unlikely that we are going to be overwhelmed by a glut of books on conscience.

This is not my first book. I have hopefully learned something about how to go about writing but the task does not seem to grow any easier. The length of time this particular project has spent on the back burner (I even have handwritten notes from pre-computer days on file) has made it particularly difficult to produce a book that is both reliable and readable. I am very grateful to Graham Hind and the team at Evangelical Press for their efforts in helping me to that end.

The writing of a book always involves the help of many, many people. Because this project has been in process for decades by now, it is difficult to remember all those to whom I am indebted for their interaction and help and to whom I should say thank you. Therefore, I simply want to thank all my friends and all my colleagues in the ministry, the church that meets in Childs Hill and, of course, my family for their patience, stimulation, contributions of books and articles and all their support. My wife and I have now been married over 25 happy years and we have become grandparents. Two of our sons currently live in Wales, two are still at home and the oldest is training for the ministry here in London.

There have been a lot of changes in my life since I first started to look at this subject. My prayer is that the things found in this book will serve to be a blessing not only to family and friends but to God's people, wherever they may be found.

Gary Brady
July 2015

Introduction

The phrase "Candle in the wind" has become very much associated in the popular mind with the late Princess Diana and, for the *cognoscenti*, with the late actress Marilyn Monroe. Matthew Henry (1662–1714) in his commentary on Romans, however, uses a similar phrase to speak of conscience. He calls it "The candle of the Lord which was not quite put out".

Others have been much more effusive about conscience. In his now famous *Les Miserables*, the French writer Victor Hugo wrote that "there is a spectacle more grand than the sea; it is heaven; there is a spectacle more grand than heaven; it is the conscience." The philosopher Immanuel Kant would often say that he knew of nothing more awe-inspiring than the starry heaven above us and conscience or moral law within us.

All sorts of people have things to say on the subject. I recently came across a statement made by the late Elvis Presley. He once observed that "when your intelligence don't tell you something ain't right, your *conscience* gives you a tap on the shoulder and says 'Hold on.' If it don't, you're a *snake*."

- What the present volume seeks to do is to bring the subject of conscience to the bar of God's Word so that we may be helped to understand it in the way that we ought to.

- The study begins by seeking to amass the biblical data. The Bible has a lot more to say on conscience, perhaps, than most people realise. Chapter 2 is an attempt to rescue the word conscience from the confusion that surrounds it and to properly define it.

- We then look at conscience in this fallen world in the unconverted, noting its strengths and weaknesses. Chapter 4 deals with the enlightened, convicted or awakened conscience and the need to preach the law. In Chapter 5, we come to the connections between the conscience and true faith and touch on the subject of assurance.

- Chapter 6 looks at the way that the Christian can and should develop his conscience, considering the good, ruling and clear conscience. Chapter 7 is on what can go wrong with conscience in the unbeliever. Here we look at the dead, the blind, the sleepy, the secure, the lukewarm, the large, the spandex (!) and the benumbed conscience.

- Chapters 8 and 9 both look at problems that arise with the consciences of Christians. We consider the strong and the weak conscience and how we should deal with differences among believers.

- In the final three chapters we tackle the interesting topics of conscience in children, conscience and religious and civil liberty and, finally, conscience in eternity.

- We have also included three appendices–on illustrations of conscience, its place in proving God's existence and some of the history of thought on the subject, especially among the Puritans.

- Books like that by Christopher Ash have been few and far between in recent years. This probably points to an underlying neglect of what is a truly important subject. It is hoped that this latest exploration of conscience will do something to help address this situation. It is intended to promote both more thought on this issue and not just more thought but more thought that is biblically informed and applied.

1 Shaking the tree
Gathering data on conscience

But the Lord God called to the man and said to him 'Where are you?' He answered, 'I heard you in the garden; I was afraid and hid from you, because I was naked.' Genesis 3:9–10

'Paul never idealises the conscience but he does call attention to it' G C Berkouwer

The Protestant Reformer Martin Luther had a great appetite for the Word of God. He once remarked that if you picture the Bible as a mighty tree and every word in it as a little branch, he had shaken every one of those branches because he wanted to know what each one was and what each one meant.

No doubt the best way to begin a study of the conscience is to go to the tree and do some shaking. We all have an idea what conscience is, of course. Everybody appears to have one. Our consciences speak to us and we can recall, perhaps, hard times it has given us. Many writers in many different fields of study have written on many different aspects of the subject. It is important, however, that all our thinking on the subject is shaped chiefly by what God's Word actually says.

In his 1956 book *The voice of conscience*, American Lutheran Alfred Rehwinkel notes how mysterious conscience is and wisely writes that 'only revelation can give us the key to this mystery'. We want to begin exploring the subject by looking at what the Bible says about conscience.

Old Testament

The Old Testament makes no direct reference to *conscience*. The Hebrews, it seems, never needed the term. This was probably because, as God's chosen people, they received direct revelation and so were, in some ways, less directly dependent on and less aware of conscience. Believing Hebrews spoke more readily of their *hearts* reflecting on revelation. 'I bless the LORD who gives me counsel; in the night also my heart instructs me' says David in Psalm 16:7. (See also Psalm 40:8, 19:11 and Ecclesiastes 7:21–22).

Adam

The *idea* of conscience certainly comes up in several places and in fact some modern translations introduce the word. The opening chapters of Genesis tell us how Adam and Eve, after they had sinned, hid in fear at the sound of the LORD God walking in the garden in the cool of the day (Genesis 3:8, 10). What is this but the earliest example of conscience at work? The Puritan William Bates wrote of Adam how after his fall 'conscience began an early hell within him'. 'Paradise with all its pleasures' he says 'could not secure him from that sting in his breast, and that sharpened by the hand of God'. He says that a consciousness of his crimes 'racked his soul with the certain and fearful expectation of judgement.'

The first instinct in all of us when sin is discovered is, like our first parents, to try and cover it up. 'For everyone who does wicked things hates the light and does not come to the light, lest his works should be exposed' (John 3:20).

Joseph and his brothers

The story of Joseph and his brothers has been singled out by several writers as one where conscience plays an important role. In Genesis 37:21-27 first Reuben, then Judah appeal to the consciences of the brothers. Reuben argues against killing Joseph. Instead of murder or any shedding of blood, he advocates throwing him into a cistern there in the desert. Judah says that they will gain nothing by killing their brother and hiding the fact and so suggests selling him to the Ishmaelites instead. He adds a direct appeal to conscience, 'for he is our brother, our own flesh.'

In the nineteenth century, Anglican theologian John King wrote of Joseph's brothers that they acted on the common fallacy that if they took suitable precautions they could effectively guard against future discovery of their crime. What they had forgotten, however, was that there was 'one witness whose eyes they could not blind, one informant whose voice they could not silence, one judge whom they were unable to bribe'. This, of course, was conscience.

Generally speaking, people tend to make no 'careful provision against the subsequent remonstrances of this monitor'. Even though they may find it difficult to overcome conscience at the beginning, they do not expect it to come haunting them after the event but very often it does.

Despite all the brothers' efforts to hide their sin, the truth eventually came out, as is so often the case. The story is quite a striking one and reminds us of how time after time God's providence can be quite remarkable. Their guilty consciences seem to have slept for many a long year (like a time bomb waiting to explode suggests Christopher Ash). It was only when at last they were forced to travel into the very land they had sold Joseph into and to stand before their, at first unrecognised, younger brother that their consciences began to speak at a volume that could not be ignored and with an authority that could not be resisted.

Genesis 42:21 reveals how the mere mention of their youngest brother Benjamin stirs their consciences and makes them say to each other 'we are guilty concerning our brother, in that we saw the distress of his soul, when he begged us and we did not listen. That is why this distress has come upon us.'

Matthew Henry notes that 'guilty consciences are apt to take good providences in a bad sense; to put wrong meanings even upon things that make for them.'

Suddenly, the brothers vividly recollect the all-but-forgotten scene, as if it were the day before. A long time has passed but suddenly this one event, an event that took but one day of their lives, looms exceedingly large and they see the replay in high definition and hear it in surround sound with the button set to replay. What King calls 'the imperishable records of conscience' are now unexpectedly and unwillingly brought to light. Like a bolt of lightning lighting up the whole sky, conscience abruptly breaks through the dark clouds of suppression and denial.

Of course, conscience is active here before any other informant, witness or judge. It is able to connect events in its own unique way. It has the power to combine things otherwise distant, dissimilar and apparently independent of each other.

When, later, a cup is found in Benjamin's sack, they say 'What shall we say to my lord? What shall we speak? Or how can we clear ourselves? God has found out the guilt of your servants' (Genesis 44:16). This reaction is prompted not by guilt for having stolen anything but by guilt over Joseph.

When Joseph finally reveals himself, they are terrified, a terror borne of guilty consciences (Genesis 45:3). Even after reconciliation, when Jacob dies, they are again fearful (Genesis 50:15). Ash refers to guilty conscience casting 'a long shadow'.

Joseph himself had suffered quite a bit since they had sold him into Egypt but one burden he had never needed to carry was that of a guilty conscience. He knew he did not deserve to be suffering as he was. What peace and comfort that must have given. What condemnation his brothers must have felt even before this point.

When Joseph himself was tempted to sin at one point, he stood firm because he kept conscience on the throne. He wisely traced the likely consequences of sin and responded to Potiphar's wife with a sincere and wise 'how then could I do this great wickedness and sin against God?' (Genesis 39:9b).

King writes of how much of sin's sting lies in the recollections of awakening conscience. Suddenly the enchantment is broken, the illusion is over, as conscience wakes, 'like a giant from his slumber' and the individual is forced to hear accusations it cannot answer and reproofs it cannot repel.

Other examples

There are other places in the Old Testament where *conscience* is clearly in mind. Job says 'I hold fast my righteousness and will not let it go; my heart does not reproach me for any of my days.' (Job 27:6). Abimelech tells God 'I have done this with a clear conscience and with innocent hands' and God replies, 'Yes, I know that you have done this with a clear conscience, ...' (Genesis 20:5–6, NET Bible). In Exodus, the hardening of Pharaoh's heart relates to the matter of conscience. Moses own conscience is seen to be at work in Exodus 2 when, having killed an Egyptian, he is distraught to find that his act had been seen. Passages in Leviticus 4 and 5 about becoming aware of sin allude to conscience and it is probably a bad conscience that made the people flee and cry out that the earth was going to swallow them, when in the desert the earth split and swallowed up a number of rebels against Moses (Numbers 16).

On at least two occasions we see David's conscience at work. We read how he was conscience-stricken both for having cut off a corner of Saul's robe (1 Samuel 24:5) and after counting the fighting men (2 Samuel 24:10). Also see 1 Samuel 25:31.

Similarly, in Psalms 32, 38 and 51, conscience is seen to be active. Psalm 32:3–4 is highly descriptive of the pangs of a bad conscience,

> For when I kept silent, my bones wasted away through my groaning all day long. For day and night your hand was heavy upon me; my strength was dried up as by the heat of summer.

Psalm 38:3–5 is similar. Psalm 51:10 expresses David's desire for a good conscience, 'Create in me a pure heart, O God, and renew a right spirit within me'.

It was on the basis that every man has a conscience that the Law was given and the prophets preached. A striking example is seen in the way Nathan dealt with David following his adultery with Bathsheba (1 Samuel 12).

Some issues are debatable—such as the role of the conscience in man as originally created in God's image. What was the significance for conscience of the knowledge of good and evil? Puritan Richard Bernard asserts that conscience was in Adam but it was not active then as it was later. His conscience witnessed to his goodness, bore sway so that he was obedient and gave him joy in God's presence. Bernard suggests that conscience will function in a similar way in the glory of heaven.

There may be references to conscience in other places in the Old Testament such as 1 Kings 8:38, Proverbs 20:27, 28:1. The Greek translation of Ecclesiastes 10:20 uses the word but it is generally accepted that this is an unhelpful translation.

New Testament

The Gospels

Turning to the New Testament, we find that the Gospels again make no direct reference to conscience. John 8:9 is dubious for several reasons that we cannot consider here. Nevertheless, the conscience is seen to be active in the story itself in John 8:1–9 as, following Jesus' statement that the first stone should be thrown by the one without sin, that is without sin in the area of adultery, people began to go away one at a time, prompted no doubt by their consciences, the older ones leaving first, until only Jesus was left, with the woman herself.

In the Gospels, as with the Old Testament, there is again reason to believe that, even where the word conscience is not used, there are occasions when the Lord Jesus has it in mind. For example, when he asks, 'And why do you not judge for yourselves what is right?' (Luke 12:57) his appeal is to conscience. Some suggest that Matthew 6:22–23, which refers to having a single or healthy eye, is talking about conscience. And what is a *pure heart* but an undefiled conscience? In Mark 3:5 Jesus rails on the stubborn hearts or hardened consciences of the Pharisees. The meaning of John 1:9 is controversial even among Reformed and Evangelical writers but Calvin and others may well be right to see conscience as at least partly the reference.

Paul and also Peter

Most New Testament references to conscience are made by Paul. In fact, of the 30 or so that exist, around 21 are in his letters (three in Romans, twelve in the Corinthian correspondence and six in the letters to Timothy), two in sermons by him found in Acts (23:1, 24:16) and five in Hebrews (9:9, 14; 10:2, 22; 13:8), which if not by Paul certainly reflects his style. The only other person to use the word is Peter, in his first letter (1 Peter 3:16, 21).

It is very much Paul's word, then. But where did he get it? Some suggest that it was a specialist word taken over from the

Stoic philosophers but it has been demonstrated to have been an everyday word among the Greeks, going back, in one form or another, to at least the sixth century BC. In his 1955 study *Conscience in the New Testament* C. A. Pierce suggests it was a *catchword* in the Corinthian church taken up by Paul and used not just in correspondence with them but, subsequently, as part of his Christian vocabulary. Certainly Paul and other New Testament writers took up Greek words and filled them with Christian meaning. Paul appears to have used the word *Saviour* in this way and Peter does this sort of thing more than once.

The New Testament, like the Old, is perfectly able to speak about conscience without using the actual word. In 1 John 3:19–21 the word *heart* is used where the word *conscience* would fit equally well.

> By this we shall know that we are of the truth and reassure our heart before him; for whenever our heart condemns us, God is greater than our heart, and he knows everything. Beloved, if our heart does not condemn us, we have confidence before God.

As we shall see, when we speak of conscience, we are really speaking of an aspect of the heart or soul, though the word is useful for speaking of a specific function of the soul, namely its moral workings.

Romans 2:14–15

The nearest the New Testament comes to any sort of definition of conscience is in Romans 2:14–15.

> For when Gentiles, who do not have the law, by nature do what the law requires, they are a law to themselves, even though they do not have the law. They show that the work of the law is written on their hearts, while their conscience also bears witness, and their conflicting thoughts accuse or even excuse them

A number of things emerge from these verses.

Firstly, everyone has a conscience, even pagans. The conscience belongs to man as man.

Secondly, these verses help us distinguish the various elements involved in making a moral decision. Although the word *conscience* is sometimes used in a general way to refer to the whole business of making moral decisions, there are, in fact, at least three clearly identifiable strands in the process.

1. The requirements of the Law of God, which are written on every man's heart.

2. The conscience itself which makes its judgements on the basis of the preceding element.

3. A man's thoughts or opinions. These come as he makes a decision on the basis of the mediation of conscience proper.

We will need to say more about Romans 2:14,15 in the next chapter. At this point, however, we have at least begun to gather the relevant material together. There is a good deal of material; more perhaps than we might have expected. This underlines the importance of the subject that we are considering.

2

What are Conscience?

Defining conscience

For when Gentiles, who do not have the law, by nature do what the law requires, they are a law to themselves, even though they do not have the law. They show that the work of the law is written on their hearts, while their conscience also bears witness, and their conflicting thoughts accuse or even excuse them.   Romans 2:14–15

'Conscience is the voice of the soul'   Polish Proverb

'What are conscience?' The question is asked by the boy puppet *Pinocchio* in Walt Disney's 1940 feature film, based on the story by Carlo Collodi. The grammar is wrong but the question is sound.

Rehwinkel observed that philosophers, psychologists and theologians down the ages have wrestled with the problem of conscience and have arrived at divergent conclusions. In any study of the subject it is good then to seek to give a clear definition of what conscience is.

Confusion

We have noted already that people are fairly familiar with the idea of conscience. They say 'my conscience is bothering me'; 'my conscience pricked me' or claim to have acted 'in good conscience'. They know what it is to have something 'on their conscience'. They know about a bad or a guilty conscience and, hopefully, a good one too.

Pierce has pointed out, however, that 'of the number that make use of the word 19 in 20 perhaps may be ignorant of its true meaning'. This is no exaggeration. Think how other Bible words are employed in everyday language. People still speak, for example, of a thing being 'as ugly as sin' or of being 'more sinned against than sinning' but how often is the word understood in the biblical sense of falling short of what God requires? It is similar with the word *conscience*.

Confusion over what exactly conscience may be is not something new either. In the seventeenth century a good number of books were written on the subject and several authors remark on this aspect. Westminster Divines John Jackson and Robert Harris, for example, speak of it having 'a thousand definitions and descriptions' it being 'a word of infinite latitude and great dispute' and 'much talked of, but little known'. Other Puritans similarly observe the difficulty of definition.

There is evidence to suggest that in many ages the word has been given such a wide range of meaning in everyday language that, though people are familiar with it, they rarely gave it an accurate biblical definition.

Writers on conscience disagree, for example, on whether to think of it primarily as a human faculty or power, an act or habit or a created quality.

If it is found in the human soul, where is it found? The understanding, the will or where? Surely it is something we can speak of as distinct from these. Not only do we tend to distinguish it from them but so does the New Testament. 1 Timothy 1:5 distinguishes conscience from the heart; Titus 1:15 distinguishes it from the mind. In experience too, conscience demonstrates an independence not observed in those other faculties.

Clarification—Etymology

The New Testament Greek word is *syneidesis*, which appears to be made up of two parts. First, *syn* or *sun* suggests *with* or *together*. *Syn*chronised swimmers co-ordinate their movements *with* each other, a *sym*phony is performed by a number of instruments playing *together* at the same time. The second part, *eidesis*, is from one of the Greek words for *to know*.

Conscience enables a certain knowledge—not the usual sort found in the understanding but a reflective knowledge over and above mere head knowledge. Richard Bernard defines it as

> a certain, particular, applicatory knowledge in man's soul, reflecting upon himself, concerning matters between God and him.

The root meaning, then, seems to be *to know together, joint knowledge* or *knowledge shared (with another)*. The Anglo-Saxon word for conscience *inwit* suggests inward knowledge but the Latin based word that superseded it, as in the romance languages, is from *con-scientia* and is made up in exactly the same way as the Greek. Other European languages, though not all, are similar. For example, Welsh *cydwybod*, Swedish *samvete*, Russian *sovest*.

This does not bring us directly to a biblical definition as there has been much debate over who shares the *joint knowledge*. Obviously, on one side is the person himself, but who is on the other? Many assume it must be God, a teaching often attributed to Augustine and taught by many others, including several Puritans, nineteenth-century Romantic poets and Roman Catholic writers old and new.

American philosopher and convert to Rome, Peter Kreeft, for example, has written of it as 'the voice of God in the soul'.

The only biblical arguments advanced for this view are dubious references to Elijah's *still small voice* and appeals to 1 Peter 2:19, 'For it is commendable if someone bears up under the pain of unjust suffering because they are conscious of God' (NIV). However, Peter clearly has in mind only Christians.

Some suggest that the word's etymology proves conscience must reveal a knowledge shared with God. Thus we have definitions such as that first given in 1933 by Norwegian theologian Ole Hallesby 'that knowledge or consciousness by which man knows he is conforming to the moral law or will of God'. While not without merit, such definitions are premature and potentially misleading.

Clarification—Usage

In his infamous *Satanic Verses* the novelist Salman Rushdie wrote that 'names, once they are in common use, quickly become mere sounds, their etymology being buried, like so many of the earth's marvels, beneath the dust of habit.' It is certainly unwise to define a word in light only of etymology. The way a word is *used* is far more important. *September* is no longer our seventh month. *Sincerity*, is literally 'without wax' but that does not help us see its meaning.

There is some disagreement about the usage of the word *syneidesis* and related words. It is clear, nevertheless, that when the

Greeks used this and related terms, it was not always in the context of *moral* judgements.

In Kittel's *Theological Dictionary of the New Testament* Christian Maurer points out a famous example where Socrates' young disciple Alcibiades speaks of being *conscious* that he could put up no resistance to the power of his teacher's arguments. There is no moral element involved. Least of all, in Greek thought, is there any necessary connection between conscience and God.

Even in the New Testament we find a related word being used in a context where conscience is clearly not intended. Acts 5:2 tells us that Ananias *with his wife's full knowledge* kept back money from the Apostles, while claiming it had been handed over. The word is *synoida*, 'to know with another'. Ananias knew what he was doing and his wife knew too.

Then in Acts 12:12 and 14:6 the ESV speaks of how Peter 'realised' and how Paul and Barnabas 'learned' a thing (the NIV speaks of the thing dawning on Peter and being found out by Paul and Barnabas). Words from the same family are again used. At their most basic, then, such words can simply mean 'to become conscious of', 'to realise'.

Most interesting in this connection is Hebrews 10:2 where the ASV speaks of worshippers who 'would have had no more consciousness of sins'. The word used is the same as that found in verse 22, *having our hearts sprinkled to save us from a guilty* conscience (NIV—The TCNT has ... *purified by the sprinkled blood from all consciousness of wrong*). In 10:2 it is really only the addition of the words 'for their sins' that brings in the moral element.

Concise Definitions

Several Puritans, tending to lean to a greater or lesser extent on the Medieval theologian Thomas Aquinas, attempted to define conscience concisely. For example

> A man's judgement of himself, according to the judgement of God of him. *William Ames*

> A part of the understanding in all reasonable creatures determining of their particular actions either with them or against them. *Samuel Ward, following William Perkins*

> The judgement of man upon himself as he is subject to God's judgement. *William Fenner*

Like Ames, Fenner refers to 1 Corinthians 11:31, which he uses more simply to say, harking back to Perkins, that conscience is 'a man's true judgement of himself'.

For the Puritans the conscience is, as Jim Packer sums it up,

> a rational faculty, a power of moral self-knowledge and judgement, dealing with questions of right and wrong, duty and desert, and dealing with them authoritatively, as God's voice.

From what we have already said, however, it is clear that we must not think of the conscience as a *department* of man's personality or a *faculty* of his soul. It can be useful to speak in such terms for the purpose of study but it is important to realise that, in reality, conscience is simply one aspect of man's personality, one function of his soul.

We have also seen that the 'joint knowledge' is not necessarily shared with God himself. In fact, put simply, the conscience is man's power of self-reflection and, particularly, self-criticism. Rehwinkel noted that the English word *consciousness* is made up in the same way as the word *conscience*. Consciousness is 'awareness of'; *conscience,* he says, is narrower in meaning and refers to 'a moral or ethical awareness'. 'Conscience' he suggests 'is a moral consciousness accompanied by a feeling of obligation and duty.'

In 1933, writing on *The conscience and its problems*, High Churchman Kenneth E Kirk similarly reminded us that though we may write of conscience as a distinct entity, we must not forget that in fact 'conscience is myself so far as I am a moral man'. American Lutheran, Milton L Rudnick, similarly calls conscience

> the self in the process of ethical deliberation and evaluation ... It is not someone or something else working in or upon man, but the moral self at work, involving all of a man's rational and emotional faculties.

Conscience is an amazing thing, one of the elements in our

make-up that distinguishes us from animals. It is one of the things that distinguishes us from brute beasts. Hallesby calls it 'very remarkable' and Bernard suggests it is the principal part of God's image in man and what most resembles God in every man.

Conscience in Romans 2:14-15 again

Given the threefold division that we saw in Romans 2:14-15 in the last chapter, it is clear that when we use the word *conscience*, we should really restrict it to the second aspect of making moral decisions, the making of judgements on the basis of what is in the moral record.

Some would suppose that this conscience only acts in a negative, condemning way. Emil Brunner's *Divine Imperative* speaks of it as a 'sinister thing' that 'attacks man like an alien, dark, hostile power'. The Russian poet Pushkin, in his play *Miserly Knight*, called conscience

> a sharp clawed animal, which scrapes the heart ... an uninvited guest, annoying discourser, a rude creditor; and a witch, which dims the moon and graves.

This may have been the Greek view but Paul points out that there are times when even the Gentile conscience can provoke thoughts that *ex*cuse as well as *ac*cuse. The Pagan can have *a bad conscience* or *a good conscience*. Strictly speaking, of course, it is not conscience that is good or bad. We do not say a barometer is bad if it correctly predicts stormy weather; we merely say that it is accurate.

Certainly the Christian can have a good conscience, as is clear from 2 Corinthians 1:12 and 1 Timothy 1:19, for instance. Romans 2:14-15 teaches the moral responsibility of all men. Walter Chantry has observed that

> Conscience alone has witnessed sufficiently to the moral law, so that everyone is without excuse. Since the fall man's heart has become a moral battleground.

Complexity

It is important not to think of conscience simplistically. Perkins talks of mind and memory assisting it, one being the storehouse and the keeper of rules and principles and the other the recaller of omissions and commissions. John Bunyan, in his *The Holy War* is quite elaborate. Bernard calls it a Director or Judge in the understanding and a Register and Secret Witness in the memory. It also works in the will, heart and affections. All the other faculties work with this one 'as it commands the whole man in the execution of its offices'. Many Puritans pictured it as a court where the roles of registrar, witnesses, prosecutor, judge and executioner are all carried out by conscience.

Such pictures are fine, provided that we remember the mysteries involved. The workings of conscience include the whole process of perceiving the requirements of God's Law, assessing them, then deciding how to proceed or what judgement to give. The overriding impression is one of 'ought' or 'ought not' but includes a whole host of mental perceptions and emotional feelings—comprehension of right and wrong; use of memory, mind and will; complacency or disquiet; shame or pride; delight or pain; anticipation of reward or punishment.

The sheer breadth of mental and emotional interplay involved can be gauged from the array of legitimate illustrations employed by different writers trying to bring out the varied character of conscience. These include spy, watchdog, bloodhound, window, mirror, sundial, compass, barometer, plumbline, sail, lash, sword, alarm bell, GPS system, flight recorder or black box and sense of taste.

Characteristics

In his book *Pure Joy* Christopher Ash has helpfully singled out five features of conscience. The list will help us to draw things together at this point.

1. Conscience speaks with a voice that is independent of us. We are able to stand outside of ourselves and look at ourselves objectively. Hallesby speaks of 'a sort of doubling of our personality'. We are, in a sense, able to stand outside ourselves and pronounce judgement on ourselves. We are able to some extent to offer an objective and unbiased judgement of ourselves.

2. Conscience speaks with a voice that looks backward and

forward. Indeed, the judgements of conscience can concern past, present or future. In this latter role conscience acts more like a guide than a judge. Hallesby observes how it is generally at its weakest during sin, in the present, but at its strongest after the event is past.

3. Ash's third observation is that other people can appeal to my conscience, as Paul does in Romans 13:5 when he tells believers that they must submit to the powers that be, not only because they may be punished but also 'for the sake of conscience'.

4. His fourth point is that God can appeal to my conscience. We have previously quoted Luke 12:57, but Ash gives Isaiah 5:3–4 as another example. There God, referring to Israel as a vineyard, says

> And now, O inhabitants of Jerusalem and men of Judah, judge between me and my vineyard. What more was there to do for my vineyard, that I have not done in it? When I looked for it to yield grapes, why did it yield wild grapes?

5. The final point is that one does not need a Bible to hear the voice of conscience. To illustrate, Ash notes how Joseph rejected the invitations to her bed extended by Potiphar's wife down in Egypt (Genesis 39). Even before the law was given, Joseph knew that adultery was wrong. Ash's other example is from the opening chapters of Amos where the surrounding nations are declared guilty not on the basis of the law but that of accepted morality.

Conclusion

In his commentary on 2 Corinthians, Puritan Richard Sibbes asks *what is conscience, but the soul itself reflecting upon itself?* He says it is 'the property of the reasonable soul and the excellency of it, that it can return upon itself.' A catechism prepared by the Scots theologian Samuel Rutherford (c 1600–1661) similarly speaks of conscience as 'the principal part of the soul'. When we speak of the workings of conscience, then, we are speaking, clearly, of *the moral workings of the soul itself.*

Despite what rationalists may have us believe, the conscience is not the result of evolution or a mere interiorisation of cultural norms or social mores. The conscience undoubtedly bears witness to the culture and morality around about us but this in no way explains its origin or function.

It is not 'the divine spark' or 'the voice of God' as such. C. H. Spurgeon once warned that there is no more atrocious mistake made by divines than when they tell people that conscience is God's representative in the soul.

Having said this, we must say that it is important to listen to its voice for it is what Christian Reformed minister Raymond Opperwall correctly called

> the internalised voice of those whose judgement of a person counts with him. It is the inner voice that testifies for the moral authorities that we recognise.

Conscience is not the voice of God in a person but that person's own voice. It is, says Rehwinkel, 'man himself speaking as a moral being to himself'. It is God given and cannot be removed. God himself has ordained and fixed it as a monitor within. We do not always like the witness conscience bears. Sometimes we disagree with it. We must all realise, however, that the voice of conscience must not be ignored. You must listen to your soul within.

3 Candle in the Wind
The unconverted conscience

... by the open statement of the truth plainly we would commend ourselves to everyone's conscience in the sight of God. 2 Corinthians 4:2

'A clear conscience is the sure sign of a bad memory' Mark Twain

In his novel *Huckleberry Finn* Mark Twain's character speaks about his conscience more than once. In Chapter 33 he says

... I warn't feeling so brash as I was before, but kind of ornery, and humble, and to blame, somehow—though I hadn't done nothing. But that's always the way; it don't make no difference whether you do right or wrong, a person's conscience ain't got no sense, and just goes for him anyway. If I had a yaller dog that didn't know no more than a person's conscience does I would poison him. It takes up more room than all the rest of a person's insides, and yet ain't no good, nohow. Tom Sawyer he says the same.

In the introduction to this book we have drawn attention to how Matthew Henry writes of conscience as 'the candle of the Lord which was not quite put out'. It is not God's voice as such but the conscience, along with the requirements of the moral law in the heart and with the mind deliberating, is a good gift from God to all human beings.

However, as Huck Finn, Tom Sawyer and many others have found, it appears to have no sense. Rehwinkel observed, in more theological terms, how 'this mysterious faculty in man' is not only 'the most sublime' but also 'one of the most perplexing problems of human existence'. The root of this problem lies in the fact that, like every other good gift from God, conscience is affected by mankind's fall into sin.

Conscience has been spoken of as a little spark of celestial fire and as God's deputy or vicegerent. It is a spark but only a little spark. It is a sort of deputy or vicegerent but a fallible one at best. Episcopalian writer Peter Toon put it this way 'your conscience is your capacity for hearing God's voice rather than being God's voice itself'.

Categories

Who has a conscience? Is it proper to speak of God as having one, as Sibbes does in one place? Perkins denies it. It is generally agreed that all human beings have a conscience. Fenner's first proposition in his book on conscience is *That everyone has a conscience*. He easily demonstrates this from the Bible. Man was created with a conscience and though now fallen it is still present in each person. Romans 2:15 and 2 Corinthians 4:2 establish this. When we speak about a person having 'no conscience' we really mean it is not working properly.

Robert Solomon suggests that the way a polygraph or lie detector can sometimes detect lying by measuring physical responses such as sweating and a racing pulse supports the view that we all have consciences.

If we want to state it very cautiously, we may say that 'conscience exists in reasonable creatures' or 'in the reasonable soul'—that is in men and angels, including fallen ones (see Revelation 19:10, James 2:21) but not animals. Some detect a shadow of it in animals but this is a misunderstanding of how conscience works. Professor John Murray was on safer ground when he apparently objected to a woman calling her cat *naughty* for catching a mouse.

Corruption

Dutch theologian G. C. Berkouwer, writing on the doctrine of man, insists that any inclination to good characteristic of the conscience is dispelled by the reality of man's inclination to evil. We can never look to conscience as something which enables man to retain a relative goodness in a special organ standing outside the effects of corruption.

Jonathan Edwards similarly spoke of natural conscience as being 'as it were, in God's stead, as an internal judge' but argued strongly in many places for the biblical doctrines of original sin and total depravity. Preaching on Hosea 5:15, he says that 'natural conscience remains, but sin, in a great degree, stupefies it, and hinders it in its work.' And so it is better to speak of conscience as a sometimes distant echo of God's voice. In the nineteenth century American Baptist D.W. Faunce reminded us that

> Conscience is not God—it is only part of one's self. To build up a religion about one's conscience as if it were God is only a refined selfishness.

Spurgeon similarly denies that conscience is 'one of those powers which retains its ancient dignity and stands erect amidst the fall of its compeers'. He says, rather,

> My Brethren, when man fell in the garden, manhood fell entirely. There was not one single pillar in the temple of manhood that stood erect. It is true, conscience was not *destroyed*. The pillar was not shattered. It fell, and it fell in one piece, and here it lies alone—the mightiest remnant of God's once perfect work in man. But that conscience is fallen, I am sure.

Conscience is not the single virtue untainted by the Fall. Every faculty in every person is affected by the sin of our father Adam. We are separated from God. His image in man has been defaced, shattered. Like all God's other gifts, conscience is misused, abused and defective. This is true also of the record of God's requirements on our hearts and our capacity to think correctly.

This is no doubt why Paul in 1 Corinthians 4:3–4 could say

> But with me it is a very small thing that I should be judged by you or by any human court. In fact, I do not even judge myself. For I am not aware of anything against myself, but I am not thereby acquitted. It is the Lord who judges me.

The Corinthians were probably quite shocked by this language as they appear to have had a very high view of conscience. Paul, however, knew his Old Testament and realised that the heart is easily deceived (Jeremiah 17:9) and that 'there is a way that seems right to a man, but its end is the way of death' (Proverbs 14:12). Conscience is not always reliable. A man can think himself innocent when he is actually guilty. He can also think himself guilty when he is actually innocent. There are psychological factors too that can sometimes mean that a person's conscience leads him astray. Even without that, fallen conscience can be easily misled.

Rutherford's catechism identifies several defects in conscience. It says of conscience

Often it is blind and dead through presumption and want of God's fear ... Often it maketh men think the way to hell is the right way, and turneth a dumb dog, that barketh not at the coming of the thief.

It also speaks evocatively of the underlying causes of these defects as ignorance of God and

... the loud crying of affections sent out to woo a wife to Satan, casting an uncouth sound in the ears and mist in the eyes of conscience.

Conceptions of right and wrong in the unconverted

When Paul says in Romans 2:15 that the Gentiles have the requirements of God's Law written on their hearts, he cannot be suggesting that each individual is born with an innate and thorough knowledge of God's Law. If that were so there would have been no need for the revelation at Sinai. Paul is not holding up the very limited conformity of the Gentiles as a moral example. The point he is driving towards is that 'none is righteous, no not one' (Romans 3:10).

Calvin says that the Ten Commandments are 'in a manner, dictated to us by an inner law, which ... is in a manner written and stamped on every heart'. That *in a manner* is important. In his commentary on Romans, John Murray points out that what Paul specifically states is that the *requirements* of the Law (literally the work or business of the law) are written in people's hearts. In other words, everyone has some idea of right and wrong, but not necessarily a very clear idea of God's holy law as written down.

Even if a fallen man's conscience functioned perfectly, it would not be bearing witness to a full and accurate record of God's commands. Thus in Bunyan's *Holy War*, we read that *Mr Mind* had only 'some old and rent and torn parchments of the law of good Shaddai in his house'.

We should not be surprised, therefore, on occasion, to hear of people, on the one hand, excusing and defending themselves for things such as murder, idolatry and immorality, things clearly contrary to God's Law and, on the other, condemning themselves for eating meat or travelling in a motorised vehicle or missing Mass, things not forbidden in the Law.

Conscience itself is a witness not a lawmaker. It can only act on the evidence available and the known law. It is a *means of knowledge* not a source for it. It refers us back to our own moral standard and urges us, with varying strength, to comply. If our moral standards are faulty, it will be impossible even to begin to offer proper obedience to God.

Conscience proper in the unconverted

The conscience itself is also imperfect, of course. It is not totally useless but it is unreliable. It can be variable, deceived, corrupted, intermittent or simply unable to cope with complex issues. Bunyan has *Mr Conscience* as the town recorder. After the fall of the town of

Mansoul he would have terrible fits at times when he would 'make the whole town of Mansoul shake with his voice' and yet at other times he would say nothing at all.

Considerations of the unconverted

Further, when conscience's faulty message is assessed in a person's thoughts, he often suppresses its message or finds other ways of ignoring it. In *Holy War* terms *Mansoul* becomes convinced that *Mr Conscience* is mad and not worth listening to. We see 'the whole town in a rage and fury against the old gentleman'. 'Yea' says Bunyan 'the rascal crew at some times would be for destroying of him'.

Collaborator and Spy

Having pointed to some of the defects in conscience, it is important to say that nevertheless the conscience is there and does function to some extent. Everyone has a moral awareness. All realise that there is right and that there is wrong. The beginning of Paul's argument in the letter to the Romans makes clear that even unbelievers know that there is a God, a God who will judge them concerning right and wrong. Therefore, even though the information available to the conscience is incomplete, nevertheless, 'the echo of the voice of God' does reach them. The voice is not as loud or as clear as before the Fall but it is there, anticipating what the eighteenth century Anglican apologist Bishop Joseph Butler referred to as 'a higher and more effectual sentence which shall hereafter second and affirm its own'.

Episcopalian theologian P. E. Hughes once observed, writing on ethics, that the way unbelievers protest against indignity and injustice indicates that 'the voice of conscience has not been utterly silenced and obliterated'. It is important for believers to remember this. God has a spy in every heart, a preacher on the inside. The conscience informs every person, however imperfectly, what God thinks of him and his actions. The better informed a man's conscience, the more effective a preacher conscience will be. That is why unbelievers will often avoid reading the Bible or hearing the word preached. The preached word is 'living and active' and 'sharper than any two-edged sword' penetrating even 'to the division of soul and spirit, of joints and of marrow' as it discerns 'the thoughts and intentions of the heart' (Hebrews 4:12). People rather want to 'turn the volume down' or to 'do a deal' with conscience so that it is pacified and will not cause them too much trouble.

We can generally expect a person to have a conscience that is at least partly active. It is important for Christian evangelists and preachers and all who would witness to Christ to remember this fact. Where a person's conscience is relatively healthy, we have an ally on the inside, a fifth columnist, a double agent, as it were.

As we bear witness to the person from without so the unbeliever also receives a witness from his conscience within. Like Paul, we need to set forth the truth plainly and so 'commend ourselves to everyone's conscience in the sight of God' (2 Corinthians 4:2). We must seek to enlighten the darkened conscience of the unbeliever with the light of God's Word.

Carry on listening

Although the conscience of the unbeliever is imperfect and fallible he should be encouraged to listen to it. Like a Supreme Court judgement, the conscience speaks categorically and absolutely. There is no room for further appeal.

In each case conscience must be followed. In his *Christian Directory* when dealing with 'temptations to draw us off from duty' Richard Baxter states in Direction 27 that

> There is a dangerous error grown too common in the world, that a man is bound to do everything which his conscience telleth him is the will of God; and that every man must obey his conscience, as if it were the lawgiver of the world; whereas, indeed, it is not ourselves, but God, that is our lawgiver.

One understands his concern and he is certainly right to say that conscience is 'not appointed or authorised to make us any duty, which God hath not made us; but only to discern the law of God, and call upon us to observe it.'

However, to then conclude that 'an erring conscience is not to be obeyed' is to introduce unhelpful complications. Yes, an erring conscience does need to be 'better informed, and brought to a righter performance of its office' but ignoring it will not bring that about. Surely Luther was on better ground when he famously said that to act against conscience is 'neither right nor safe' as was Matthew Henry when he said that 'we must never be overawed, either by majesty or multitude, to do a sinful thing, and to go against our consciences'.

Commenting on Romans 2, Dr Martyn Lloyd-Jones, while admitting conscience's imperfection, was emphatic

> Nevertheless we should always obey it. 'Ah, yes', you may say, 'but your conscience may be unenlightened'. If that is so, then it is my business to subject myself to further teaching. A conscience can be feeble, it can be unenlightened, and I can educate it, I can teach it and train it; but whatever state my conscience may be in, it is never right for me to do anything against it.

Certainly following conscience does not guarantee good and it is more grievous to sin by going against conscience than by obeying it. There is a dilemma in this area, of course, what R.C. Sproul once dubbed 'the double jeopardy dilemma'. If we follow conscience into sin we are guilty, yet to act against conscience is not right either. Meanwhile, rather than subverting its authority we must correct abuses of conscience. King says astutely '*conscience is a monarch* which needs to be trained for the elevated post it has to fill'.

This is not to buy into the Roman Catholic idea of invincible ignorance, the teaching that a person is not guilty of sin if they act in ignorance. Rather, it is to stress how vital it is for everyone to conform what is in their moral record to what is found in the Bible itself concerning God's will. Jiminy Cricket's sung advice to 'always let your conscience be your guide' is fine as far as it goes. Our cartoon grasshopper ought to have sung 'always let your conscience be informed by the revealed will of God and be your guide!'

It is not enough to set your watch by the kitchen clock, you must also be sure that the clock is set to the astronomical standards of time. Charles Gore, first Bishop of Birmingham, had it right when he said that 'man's first duty is not to follow his conscience but to enlighten his conscience'. Do not waste time and cause damage by endeavouring to get anyone to act against his conscience. Concentrate rather on making sure that his mind is properly informed by God's Word.

To quote John King once again

> though conscience may be deceived, yet it is not on that account to be deprived of its office, but rather to be instructed, strengthened, fortified and improved, so as to be duly fitted for functions, which no other faculty of the mind can possibly discharge.

Content

We see then why in his famous interview with Mary, Queen of Scots, the godly Reformer John Knox could say to her that her conscience was useless while it was not properly informed.

'Conscience, Madam,' said he 'requireth knowledge; and I fear that right knowledge ye have none'. What matters so much is the content of the moral standard to which conscience bears witness. 'How well do I know the requirements of God's Law?' That is the vital question.

The nineteenth century Baptist theologian A. H. Strong points out that conscience itself can only be educated 'in the sense of acquiring greater facility and quickness in making decisions'. In his book on *Ethics* Dietrich Bonhoeffer spoke of people in his day who said, 'Adolf Hitler is my conscience' meaning that the Fuhrer dictated their moral standard. The appalling ramifications of such a statement are now obvious to all. Rather, as Bonhoeffer says, people should say, 'Jesus Christ is my conscience'.

To put it another way, the high court of conscience is not the highest court. We have already quoted 1 Corinthians 4:4 and Paul's statement that a clear conscience does not make a person innocent. The Apostle is a notorious example, before his conversion, of a conscience that excused actions anything but pleasing to God. See Philippians 3:4-6 where Paul acknowledges his zeal for persecuting Christians and John 16:2 where Jesus predicts such things. As Reformed theologian Herman Ridderbos notes, the reference here is not so much to the inadequacy of conscience, as the older Reformed commentators point out, but to the importance of the coming judgement. What matters is God's verdict, not ours. Nevertheless the imperfect nature of the conscience does come out here and ought to be remembered. The judgement of conscience does not signal the end of all dispute.

The conscience is usually consistent, although never infallible. A healthy conscience is not easily fooled. Like the proverbial mule, it is a stubborn creature. It will not be easily swayed by popular opinion or fear of danger. Obstinate, persistent and often inflexible, conscience is a good friend to have when it is right but a real handicap when it is wrong. A misinformed conscience can lead you into trouble and do a great deal of damage. It is something like a magnetic compass. While the needle points to magnetic north, all is well but if at some stage one enters a strong magnetic field that is not the earth's own then disaster may well follow for anyone relying on that compass. Following your nose is a good way to get to a place but first you have to point your nose in the right direction!

Controvertible

The conscience is certainly persistent. It can pursue a person for crimes committed decades ago. The memory of offences minor or major can haunt a person for years. The case of Katherine Ann Power is of interest in this respect. In 1993 the 44 year old Oregon resident, then calling herself Alice Metzinger, handed herself in to the authorities, confessing that 23 years before, as a student, she had taken part in armed bank robberies in Massachusetts. The robberies were intended to raise money for political activities. In 1970 she and an accomplice had been on the FBI's most wanted list but she was never arrested. After her belated confession she served six years in detention before her release on 14-years' probation. What prompted her confession? Her inability to live with a guilty conscience, especially as in one robbery a police officer had been killed. She said in court

> His death was shocking to me, and I have had to examine my conscience and accept any responsibility I have for the event that led to it.

The words 'the torture of a bad conscience is the hell of a living soul' are often attributed to Calvin. He certainly said that 'the gnawing of a guilty conscience, tormented by the dread of the Divine judgement, may be compared to the porch of hell.' Spurgeon commented that he would rather bear any affliction than the burden of a guilty conscience. Thunderbolts, tornadoes, a dark dungeon full of snakes and other reptiles, being burnt at the stake—for him, all were preferable to a burning and guilty conscience. 'Oh give me not over to my own thoughts when I am consciously guilty before God!' he says. Some people have even taken their own lives rather than live with an accusing conscience.

The conscience truly is at times an awesome force with which to reckon. Nevertheless, even a well informed conscience can be controverted. It can be resisted. If it cannot be completely ignored, it can certainly be defied. An active conscience does not guarantee anything, in and of itself. If desensitised enough, a conscience can even be hardened to the point where it hardly functions at all.

The conscience alone is inadequate to save anyone. To quote Spurgeon on depravity again

> Did any man's conscience, unenlightened by the Spirit, ever tell him that his sins deserved damnation? Or if conscience did do that, did it ever lead any man to feel an abhorrence of sin as sin? In fact, did conscience ever bring a man to such a self-renunciation that he did totally abhor himself and all his works and come to Christ? No, conscience, although it is not dead, is ruined. Its power is impaired, it has not that clearness of eye and that strength of hand and that thunder of voice which it had before the Fall. It has ceased, to a great degree, to exert its supremacy in the town of Mansoul. Then, Beloved, it becomes necessary for this very reason, because conscience is depraved, that the Holy Spirit should step in to show us our need of a Saviour and draw us to the Lord Jesus Christ.

Again we say, however, that conscience is a God-given gift that witnesses to the state of our relationship with our Maker. It is an eternal voice speaking into this temporal life, what has been called a line connecting man to his Creator or a certain mean between God and man that does not allow him to suppress within himself what he knows, but pursues him to the point of convicting him.

Every person ever created has a conscience, even the most depraved. In each case, conscience is fallible but it is still a potential ally on the inside in the war to recapture the souls of lost men and women and children. Give thanks and praise to God for the conscience!

4
Thundering beginnings
The awakened conscience

For by works of the law no human being will be justified in his sight, since through the law comes knowledge of sin. Romans 3:20

'The first effect of the voice of Christ is conviction upon the conscience; conviction both of sin and misery' John Flavel

Hallesby observes that 'conscience itself is one of the sleepiest of all things and unless God awakens it, it would never waken itself or waken us'. Because human beings are fallen, this is bound to be the case. Every individual has a conscience. There are times when its activity can be most intense, even in pagans, yet for most of the time it is more or less dormant in most people. He goes on to remind us of those times when it has failed to give expression to its judgements or when it has spoken so feebly and indistinctly that it has neither been heard nor heeded.

Mr Conscience in *The Holy War* was thrown into prison because of his opposition to the schemings of Diabolus. From its very first risings, the witness of conscience in the unconverted man is attacked and opposed.

Puritan Anthony Burgess (c 1600–1663) lamented the attempts so many make to 'put a foggy mist between their conscience and themselves' either by giving themselves to lusts and carnal pleasures or by digging into the world, 'labouring to become senseless' and seeking to eclipse the light of heaven by the interposition of the earth or else denying basic Christian doctrines and turning to heresy. All these, he tells us, are 'but refuges of guilty consciences'.

In his *Instructions about heartwork*, another Puritan, Richard Alleine, addresses the unbeliever as follows

> Dost thou make no conscience of thy ways? Hast thou slighted conscience, hast thou wounded conscience so long, that now it lets thee alone to thy will, and thy lust? Or, if it checks thee sometimes, for thy evils, yet thou bearest it down, and goest on thy way against

its reproofs and contradictions? Art thou a man of no conscience? Is it not against thy conscience to lie, or to defraud, or to drink to drunkenness, to live without praying or minding God or thy soul? Does conscience let thee alone to live thus? Or, if it doth smite thee, yet goest thou still on against it? Art thou a man of no more conscience than this? What dost thou think of thyself? Whatever thou thinkest, thou art a lost soul: while conscience is lost, thy soul is lost. Till conscience be recovered, thy soul is not recovered: and conscience is never recovered, till it hath recovered its authority, and hath gotten the rule and the government of thee.

Such a conscience, he says, is 'as a city that hath neither gates nor bars, but is left open to the devil, in which to rule at his pleasure'. 'God hath not recovered the rule of any soul' he asserts 'till conscience be awakened and hath recovered its authority'.

Law inadequate

In some cases, it is not that there is a lack of accurate information in the moral record with which to come to a right verdict. In Romans 2:13 Paul makes clear that there are many who know God's Law. Of itself this cannot help them, however. Why?

> For it is not the hearers of the law who are righteous before God, but the doers of the law who will be justified.

In many countries there have been people with a fairly accurate knowledge of God's Word who, nevertheless, seem largely unaffected by it. Their consciences are unable to make them conform to what the divine light reveals. They feel urged but not compelled and so make bad choices and in due time suffer the consequences.

It is tempting to imagine that mere exposure to God's Holy Word will automatically bring about conviction of sin and a turning to God. This is patently not the case. As we have said, the conscience, including the moral record and the mind, is fallen. It does not function as it should. It is defective, insensitive and apathetic. It repeatedly lets us down. Even with a clear testimony to God's Law it is unable to change a person's heart. In other words, man cannot convert himself. As the tenth article of the Church of England begins

> The condition of Man after the fall of Adam is such, that he cannot turn and prepare himself, by his own natural strength and good works, to faith; and calling upon God.

We have already quoted Jeremiah 17:9 which reminds us that 'the heart is deceitful above all things and beyond cure'.

Heart illuminated, awakened and convicted

Before the conscience can gain any benefit from an accurate revelation, God must perform the miracle of illumination, awakening or conviction. The words can be used interchangeably, although there is some merit in understanding them in the following way.

Illumination may refer chiefly to the way that the Spirit enlightens the moral record so that it focuses on the Word.

Awakening may refer chiefly to what happens in the conscience proper so that it begins to function as it should.

Conviction may refer chiefly to the effect on the mind of a person as they come to realise in their thinking that they have sinned against God and are guilty before him.

Normally, the conscience can be easily pacified—excuses, a few good deeds, some pre-occupation with pleasure. However, once conscience is illuminated and the heart is awakened and convicted, it is not so easy to mollify one's conscience.

Spiritual awakening affects the whole person but undoubtedly shows itself first and foremost in the conscience. Jonathan Edwards wrote of conviction in his sermon on Hosea 5:15, already quoted

> No new principle is infused. Natural men have only natural principles; and therefore all that is done by the Spirit of God before regeneration is by assisting natural principles. ... the principle which is assisted in making natural men sensible of their desert of wrath, is natural conscience. Though man has lost a principle of love to God, and all spiritual principle, by the fall, yet natural conscience remains.

By one means or another God touches the conscience and it begins to function in a way that is more like its intended one. The stimulus can be one or more of any number of things—an illness, a bereavement, a serious conversation, an awakening sermon. Various circumstances may be the cause, under God, of triggering or awakening the uncocked or drowsing conscience. It can happen to an individual in isolation or to a whole family or to a whole community, even a nation. There is certainly mystery here. Why should certain things lead to conviction in some circumstances but not in others? The results of conviction are more easily observed than are the mediate causes.

Gradually, or sometimes more quickly, the convicted person is brought to see quite vividly that there is a God in heaven to whom he must one day give an account of his life. Unbidden, the conscience begins to speak in a way that it never consistently did before. At the beginning, it convicts over individual sins and eventually concerning the fact that the individual is sinful in his whole person. Edwards speaks of how, when he convinces a sinner, God assists his conscience 'against the stupefaction of sin', helping it to do its work 'more freely and fully'. God's Spirit works immediately on the conscience, convicting and awakening. This is where the convincing work goes on. 'Their consciences smite them and condemn them'. This is what we should pray for. Pray with Francis Bottome

> Throw light into the darkened cells,
> Where passion reigns within;
> Quicken my conscience till it feels
> The loathsomeness of sin.

Heart tormented

In many ways this stage in spiritual experience is a strange one. Awakening does not come because the individual seeks or desires it; it is something that God does by his Spirit. In fact there is very much an inward conflict as God's Law is brought to bear on the conscience in a very painful way.

'Conviction of sin is like a pain' wrote Baptist pastor David Fountain in a brief examination of the subject some years ago. 'It is unpleasant and we naturally protect any sore place so that the amount of pain we feel is minimal. However, pain is a precious indicator that something is wrong.'

In *The Holy War* the Captains Boanerges (conviction and judgement) beat at Mr Conscience's door so that his house trembles and totters. Bunyan writes

> As yet he knew nothing of the great designs of Emmanuel; so that he did not know what judgement to make nor what would be the end of such thundering beginnings.

All that Mr Conscience could think of was his guilt and the destruction deserved by Mansoul.

In an awakening, conscience reasserts itself. Its voice becomes stronger, more persistent, more consistent. The sinner hears the voice of God in his Word, he senses God's eye is on him. He often feels that God is watching him every moment of the day and night. In Calvin's words, the 'lurking and lagging conscience' is compelled to utter 'all things that have even now been forgotten'.

This sort of thing is most marked in seasons of refreshing from God when there is a general awakening in a church or in a village or town or over a wider area. Nevertheless, it will be the invariable ingredient, to a greater or lesser degree, in any true case of conviction of sin. In some cases, for the convicted, the pangs of conscience are indescribable. The sinner is brought to utter self-despair. We ought to have great sensitivity to and compassion for those who find themselves in such a position, especially when this is their state over a prolonged period of time. Calvin warns that 'nothing more readily happens to fearful consciences than falling into despair'. It has been said that there is no hell like a bad conscience and many have noted how dreadful a thing conviction of sin can be.

William Gurnall, author of the Puritan classic *Christian in Complete Armour*, wrote there that 'no torment in the world is comparable to an accusing conscience'.

An outstanding example of conviction is found in Bunyan's classic autobiography *Grace Abounding to the chief of sinners*. There he describes how it began with a sermon against Sabbath breaking by the local parson. He describes how, before this, he 'had taken much delight' in church bell ringing but now

> my conscience beginning to be tender; I thought such a practice

was but vain, and therefore forced myself to leave it, yet my mind hankered; wherefore I would go to the steeple-house and look on, though I durst not ring.

Another notable example of deep conviction is C.H. Spurgeon. We have already mentioned his preference for thunderbolts, tornadoes, a dungeon of snakes or being burnt at the stake to a guilty conscience. In a sermon in 1860 he reminisces,

> I recollect the time when I thought I had rather have been a frog or a toad than have been made a man; when I reckoned that the most defiled creature, the most loathsome and contemptible was a better thing than myself; for I had so grossly and grievously sinned against Almighty God.

On another occasion he asked 'this side of Hell, what can be worse than the tortures of an awakened conscience?'

In one of his hymns, Isaac Watts begins by describing how secure he once felt.

> Lord, how secure my conscience lay,
> And felt no inward dread!
> I was alive without the law,
> And thought my sins were dead.

Although his 'hopes of heaven were firm and bright', God's Law came in 'with a convincing power and light' and he found that in fact he was a vile wretch. He goes on

> My guilt appeared but small before,
> Till terribly I saw
> How perfect, holy, just, and pure,
> Was thine eternal law.
> Then felt my soul the heavy load,
> My sins revived again
> I had provoked a dreadful God,
> And all my hopes were slain.

Law preached

Conviction does not guarantee conversion. This is rather where the road to possible conversion really begins. For this reason, the proclaiming of the Law of God is of high importance. There is sometimes a tendency among evangelicals to downplay the Law and proceed to a straight declaration of the gospel. The Law is not allowed to have its proper place. Some years ago Professor John Murray wrote that it is a primary task of an evangelist to bring the demands of law and gospel to bear on the conscience. 'One of the most appalling defects of much present day evangelism' he says is the failure to proclaim and apply the Ten Commandments. It is as these commands are brought to bear on people's hearts and lives that the effect referred to by the Apostle Paul (Romans 7:7, 9) is produced.

'Only the sharp arrows of God's commandments' says Murray

'can pierce the hearts of the King's enemies and only these can lay low the self-sufficiency of human pride.' It is through the law, the law applied to the conscience, that we become conscious of sin (Romans 3:20). Paul says, 'For through the law I died to the law, so that I may live for God.' and, 'So then, the law was our guardian until Christ came, ...' (Galatians 2:19, 3:24).

The commandments do the vital work of killing so that a person can come to true life in Christ. They discipline a man and take charge of him in order to bring him to Christ. Hallesby is very helpful when he says,

> We should never try to make ourselves believe that we can persuade anyone to believe in the gospel before, by the grace of God, we have helped him to believe in the law of God and his will and that he must do the will of God ...

This is the order then, first law then gospel. Calvin stresses in the Institutes how we need to be cast down 'into complete consternation' for only this prepares us

> to receive Christ's grace. For he who considers himself capable of enjoying it is deceived unless he has first humbled all haughtiness of mind. This is a well known passage, *God opposes the proud but gives grace to the humble.* (1 Peter 5:5, James 4:16, see Proverbs 3:3–4)

In the seventeenth century the Anglican divine Ezekiel Hopkins wrote that

Where the Law hath not wrought its convincing work with power upon the conscience, there the preaching of Jesus Christ will be altogether in vain. For, until a sinner be thoroughly convinced of his guilt and misery; and his conscience be awakened by the threats and terrors of the Law, that he stands forfeited to the justice of God, liable to eternal wrath, and may every moment be swallowed up in the abyss of woe and torments, into which thousands before him have been already plunged; it will be impossible to persuade him seriously to embrace those tenders of mercy, which the Gospel holds forth unto him by Jesus Christ.

Puritan John Flavel puts it pithily, 'Christ is not sweet until sin be made bitter to us'. There is a need to preach both law and gospel, sin and salvation. One of the strange things about conviction of sin, it should be noted, is that even the gospel can sound like law to the person whose conscience has been awakened. It is the duty of preachers, nevertheless, to uphold and proclaim the whole counsel of God.

The instinct of the convicted sinner is to suppose that he will be made right with God through his conscience. He believes that as his conscience grows ever more sensitive and as he is ever more submissive to it, he will one day find salvation. Yet even when his conscience cries out with greater authority he still falls into sins and this can only drive him further into despair. He knows, of course, that there is such a thing as forgiveness but he also knows that it is only for those who repent and believe. But these are the very things, his conscience tells him, that he is incapable of doing properly. His faith is a sham, he feels, his repentance shallow. As it has been put 'one drop of an evil conscience troubles a whole sea of outward comforts'. How can he escape from his sins? There seems to be no way out.

Heart renewed

Is there a way out? If so, what is it?

There is a way, just one way—and it is not through conscience. Berkouwer explains

> There is ... no hidden power of regeneration in conscience and we may not at all identify conscience and repentance ... true repentance is not at all a mere extension of conscience. The conscience implies a protest against evil, a negative, but this does not necessarily lead to repentance ... it does not breakthrough man's alienation from God and presents no solution which can restore life's harmony.

Regeneration is what is needed, nothing less. The soul, the very nature of the person needs to be renewed. This new birth and the consequent forgiveness of sin is only possible because of the atonement secured by the Lord Jesus Christ (see Romans 3:25–26; 2 Corinthians 5:21). It is when a sinner comes to absolute self despair and the first risings of faith in the Lord Jesus Christ that we have reason to hope he is born again. Faith in Christ is the key because it is only, 'the blood of Christ, who through the eternal Spirit, offered himself without blemish to God' that can, 'purify our conscience from dead works to serve the living God.' (Hebrews 9:14)

> Jesus, my great High Priest,
> Offered his blood, and died;
> My guilty conscience seeks
> No sacrifice beside:
> His powerful blood did once atone,
> And now it pleads before the throne,
>
> Isaac Watts

Gurnall described it in terms of a sergeant or policeman,

> Conscience is God's sergeant he employs to arrest the sinner. Now the sergeant has no power to release his prisoner on any private composition between him and the prisoner, but listens, whether the debt be fully paid or the creditor be fully satisfied, then and not till then he is discharged of his prisoner.

The most that we can expect from conscience is that, under God, it will arrest us and bring us to him that he may deal with us. Although conviction is not enough to save us, it is, nevertheless, a wonderful thing indeed and something we should long for.

The Bible is clear that the only way a man's Creditor can be satisfied and the debt cleared is through the propitiation made by Christ on the cross. It is by faith in Christ and what he has done that a person is set free. This faith comes through regeneration or being born again.

That is exactly right. We must not shy away from this difficult initial task. The healing surgeon who saves lives begins his operations by wielding a sharp scalpel. You have to be cruel to be kind. 'The conscience is not to be healed if it be not wounded' as Perkins put it.

The nineteenth century German pastor F.W. Krummacher rightly pointed to the two sides of this. There is conscience like a raging sea, stirred up by the preaching of the law. It is like a gnawing worm in the bones. Calm comes only at the sign of the cross. It is only when the blood of God's Son is applied that the worm dies and the sea grows calm. Both these truths need to be proclaimed today—the wounding law and the healing gospel.

> Come, ye sinners, poor and needy,
> Weak and wounded, sick and sore;
> Jesus ready stands to save you,
> Full of pity, love and power.
> He is able,
> He is willing; doubt no more.
>
> Come, ye thirsty, come, and welcome,
> God's free bounty glorify;
> True belief and true repentance,
> Every grace that brings you nigh.
> Without money
> Come to Jesus Christ and buy.
>
> Come, ye weary, heavy laden,
> Lost and ruined by the fall;

If you tarry till you're better,
You will never come at all.
Not the righteous
Sinners Jesus came to call.

View him prostrate in the garden;
On the ground your Maker lies.
On the bloody tree behold him;
Hear him cry before he dies
'It is finished!'
Sinner, will this not suffice?

Lo! th'incarnate God ascended,
Pleads the merit of his blood
Venture on him, venture wholly,
Let no other trust intrude.
None but Jesus
Can do poor sinners good.

Let not conscience make you linger,
Nor of fitness fondly dream;
All the fitness he requireth
Is to feel your need of him.
This he gives you
'Tis the Spirit's rising beam.

Joseph Hart

5 Peace perfect peace
Believing and conscience

... wage the good warfare, holding faith and a good conscience ...
1 Timothy 1:18–19

'Q. What are the blessings which usually accompany God's justified, adopted, and sanctified ones? A. Peace of conscience, joy in the Holy Ghost, and increase of grace.' Thomas Gouge

Commenting on Hebrews 9:9–10 the great John Owen points out that 'nothing can give perfect peace of conscience with God but what can make atonement for sin'. He says that 'whoever attempts it any other way but by virtue of that atonement, will never attain it, in this world nor hereafter.'

Gurnall says more positively 'peace of conscience is but a discharge under God's hand, that the debt due to divine justice is fully paid'. He speaks of *the echo of pardoning mercy*, which sounding in the conscience, brings the soul into a sweet rest with the pleasant music it makes'.

Writing on assurance, Dr Lloyd-Jones similarly noted that 'the man who has been justified by faith and who has peace with God, can answer the accusations of his own conscience'.

As we have said, most people whose conscience is troubled usually find it relatively easy to placate or pacify it to some extent. True and lasting peace of conscience, however, is something that God alone can give. Real peace of conscience is possible only when conscience proper is convinced that justice has been done and the only just solution to the problem of man's sin is found in the atoning death of the Lord Jesus Christ as revealed to us in the Bible. True peace comes only when this is to some extent understood and believed and becomes the only ground of hope for justice and forgiveness.

Conscience and faith

There is no explicit reference to peace of conscience in the New Testament and although conscience and faith cannot really be separated there would appear to be no great stress on the role of conscience in coming to faith. Having seen, however, that the conscience is really an aspect of the heart or soul, we should recognise that verses that speak of the heart or soul are speaking, therefore, to some extent of the conscience. So when Paul says in Romans 10:10 'it is with the heart man believes' there is a sense in which we can legitimately say, 'it is with or in the conscience that man believes'.

Hallesby says

> No man possesses any other faith in God than that which springs forth from the immediate assurance of his own conscience … faith is a fruit of conscience for it is conscience which gives his consciousness of God the leading place in his personality.

He goes on to point out that conscience, unlike the intellect, never gives reasons for its judgements. Richard Bernard noted too how no person can simply work his conscience to his own will and pleasure and Lloyd-Jones spoke of it being an independent witness that can be opposed but not manipulated.

Conscience, therefore, is most suited to being the seat of faith. Faith must centre on the fact that God speaks and has to be believed not on some merely rationalistic process. Gurnall wrote that 'if faith be a jewel a good conscience is the cabinet in which it is kept.' More prosaically, theologian H. C. Hahn says conscience 'can be regarded as the place where the mystery of faith is to be found'.

All this seems to square with a number of New Testament Scriptures. In 1 Timothy 3:9 it is with a clear conscience that the deacons of the church are to keep hold of the deep truths of the faith. In 1 Timothy 4:1–2 it is those who have abandoned the faith who are said to have *seared* consciences (see also 1 Timothy 1:19).

Further, a careful comparison of the arguments Paul uses in 1 Corinthians 8 with those that he uses in the parallel passage in Romans 14 reveals that he uses the words faith and conscience almost interchangeably in the two passages. So for example when Paul speaks of 'their *conscience*, being weak' in 1 Corinthians 8:7, in Romans 14:1 it is 'the one who is weak in *faith*'. When in Romans 14:2 he says 'One person *believes* he may eat everything', the phrase 'one person's conscience says' could easily replace the opening words without any change of meaning.

Conscience and renewal

Writing on the law and adverting to what Paul speaks about in Romans 7, Lloyd-Jones says that though the conscience of the unregenerate man troubles him,

> There is *all the difference in the world between an unregenerate man* who has trouble with his conscience, and a man who is able to say 'It is no more I that do it, but sin that dwelleth in me.' In the case of the unregenerate man, the total personality of the man is 'aware' of the speaking of *conscience*, but he is united against his *conscience*. He loves sin, desires sin, and wills sin, and he wishes that he had not got a *conscience*. *He* does not 'condemn' what he is doing, *he is*

simply aware that his conscience condemns it. He is worried about something, as it were, outside himself; hence he tries, by means of psychology and everything else he can lay hold of, to get rid of this *voice of conscience. As a whole* he is against this, but the man the Apostle is describing is a *man who is divided* in himself—'It is no more *I* that do it'.

When a person becomes a Christian there are major changes for his conscience. Each of its three parts is radically transformed and so there is a major re-orientation.

Knowledge of the law

The first, though not always the most radical change, comes in the Christian's knowledge of the law. Obviously there is a graduation here from the state of things when the person was unconverted to his state when he is first illuminated and on to his state as a mature Christian. Nevertheless, at conversion there is a unique and definite change in the 'authority focus' of the conscience. The flame that burned so low and flickered so weakly and almost went out, now blazes up with a phosphoric brightness. The Law of God now becomes etched on the heart—not the *requirements of the Law* but the Law itself. These are the terms in which the promise is given in Jeremiah 31:33–34

> For this is the covenant that I will make with the house of Israel after those days, declares the LORD: I will put my law within them, and I will write it on their hearts. And I will be their God, and they shall be my people. And no longer shall each one teach his

neighbour and each his brother, saying, 'Know the LORD,' for they shall all know me, from the least of them to the greatest, declares the LORD. For I will forgive their iniquity, and I will remember their sin no more.

More clearly than at any previous point, the will of God suddenly becomes as clear as daylight in the converted conscience.

Conscience proper

As for the conscience proper, its renewal means that it now becomes a far more sensitive instrument than it ever was before. Again, one has to recognise degrees here, going back to conversion and even before that. However, once the light begins to dawn at conversion, the blinds on the window conscience open, the curtains are torn apart, never to be fully closed again. The grime of the years is polished away and at last the mirror conscience begins to reflect the light in the way that God intended. Whereas previously the conscience was often faint, sometimes erratic, and generally unreliable, it is now much more a force to depend on in the evil day. Mad Mr Conscience, in *Holy War* terms, is restored to health and is made Town Preacher!

The accusing or excusing faculty

At last, the conscience becomes what the New Testament refers to as *good* (see 1 Timothy 1:19, 1 Peter 3:21) *clear* (the implication of Hebrews 9:9) or *cleansed* (Hebrews 10:22). It accuses or excuses, attacks or defends, on adequate grounds. This is the opposite to the defiled or evil conscience spoken of in Titus 1:15 and Hebrews

10:22, the conscience weighed down by acts that lead to death (see also Hebrews 9:14).

These terms are used not only to describe the initial change at conversion but also the way a believer's conscience may be at any given time—that is, not accusing at that present moment. See 1 Timothy 1:5, 19, 3:9 and 2 Timothy 1:3, where Paul speaks of 'a pure heart and a good conscience and a sincere faith'; urges Timothy to hold on to 'faith and a good conscience'; refers to deacons holding to the deep truths of the faith 'with a clear conscience' and speaks of his conscience being clear. In 2 Corinthians 1:12 Paul declares how his own conscience testifies to his having conducted himself 'with simplicity and godly sincerity that are from God'. There is something similar in Hebrews 13:18 ('Pray for us, for we are sure that we have a clear conscience, desiring to act honourably in all things') and a call for a clear conscience in 1 Peter 3:16. Nevertheless, it is at conversion that the conscience is cleansed, cleared, perfected or made good. The load of guilt is removed, the stain is wiped out forever. The conscience begins to function as it ought to and no longer accuses in the way that it once did.

Conscience and perfection

The New Testament Letter to the Hebrews was written, it would seem, to Jewish Christians who, because of the opposition and hardship they were experiencing, were seriously thinking of going back to the Judaism from which they had apparently been delivered. The writer stresses what a retrograde step a return to

Judaism would be, if it were possible to go back to it. There is no hope of salvation for anyone in that direction. The gifts and sacrifices offered in Old Testament times (9:9) were not able to 'perfect the conscience of the worshipper'. If Old Testament sacrifices could have cleared people's consciences then they would have stopped being offered long before the Temple came to an end, subsequent to the writing of Hebrews, in AD 70.

Why? Since 'the worshippers, having once been cleansed, would no longer have any consciousness of sins' (10:2). The old covenant ritual was not intended to take away sin but to point forward to something better that would do it. Though commanded by God for his own good purposes, of themselves, they were no more able to perfect and cleanse the inner person, the conscience, than any other merely human effort. There was a way of salvation for Old Testament believers but it was never through the blood of goats and bulls. These sacrifices were only intended to make the worshipper outwardly, ritually or ceremonially clean. They could never deal with his heart and were never intended to. Their purpose, rather, was to direct his attention to what would be achieved with the death of Messiah Jesus, the Lamb slain from the foundation of the world.

'Nothing can take off conscience from accusing but that which can take God off from threatening'—Gurnall again. And so the writer to the Hebrews declares (9:14)

> How much more will the blood of Christ, who through the eternal

Spirit offered himself without blemish to God, purify our conscience from dead works to serve the living God.

All peace of conscience is resolved in the atonement, Christ's substitutionary atoning death for sinners. This alone can effectively cleanse conscience. As Thomas Baird wrote in a little book on conscience published in 1914 'Years of continued sin, unconfessed to God, eat like rust into the substance of conscience and nothing but the blood of Christ can remove the stain'. It is because of the atonement that the Christian is justified and it is justification that leads to peace of conscience.

Preaching on peace of conscience the Scottish Puritan Thomas Boston says that it is 'a benefit flowing from justification'. He describes this 'blessed inward calmness and consolation' as leaning on Abraham's breast on this side of heaven and a 'lower paradise'. 'It is like the shore to the shipwrecked soul' he says 'and life from the dead'.

It comes both from the removal of guilt and the removal of a conscience about guilt. There is both pardon (Hebrews 9:14) and a sense of pardon (Hebrews 10:2). There is calmness and comfort.

The law and conscience

Ezekiel Hopkins, looking at pardon and forgiveness, wrote

I do not say, that peace of conscience is always an inseparable attendant upon pardon of sin; for, doubtless, there are many so unhappy, as to have a wrangling conscience in their own bosoms, when God is at peace with them: but this is certain, that pardon of sin lays a solid ground and foundation for peace in a man's own conscience; and, were Christians but as industrious as they should be in clearing up their evidences for heaven, they might obtain peace whenever they are pardoned.

The subject of Christian assurance is a vast and sometimes controversial one and not one that we can go into in any detail here. It is clear, however, that the conscience should play an important part in assuring the believer that he has found the truth. In Tullian Tchividjian's words, assurance has to do 'with the conscience's confidence in ultimate acquittal before God'. It is the heart, including the conscience, that needs to be put at rest. Such rest, if it is genuine, does not come from a sleeping or dead conscience but from one that is very much awake and alive. Although it condemns us, it also recognises that 'God is greater than our hearts' and 'knows everything' (1 John 3:19-20). It is this lively Christian conscience that gives true assurance.

In his essay on 'Happiness' in his book *Practical Religion,* Bishop J. C. Ryle pointed out that real happiness comes from a conscience at peace.

The true Christian is the only happy man, because *his conscience is at peace.* That mysterious witness for God, which is so mercifully placed within us, is fully satisfied and at rest. It sees in the blood of Christ a complete cleansing away of all its guilt. It sees in the priesthood and mediation of Christ a complete answer to all its fears. It sees that through the sacrifice and death of Christ God can now be just and yet the justifier of the ungodly. It no longer bites and stings and makes its possessor afraid of himself. The Lord Jesus Christ has amply met all its requirements. Conscience is no longer the enemy of the true Christian, but his friend and adviser. Therefore he is happy.

C. H. Spurgeon, in his sermon *The purging of conscience* on Hebrews 9:13–14, speaks in similar terms.

> We read *the blood of Jesus Christ his Son cleanseth us from all sin* and our conscience whispers 'we are cleansed from all sin!' Conscience finds rest and peace and our whole consciousness becomes that of a forgiven and accepted person with whom God is well pleased. Our conscience, instead of condemning us, perceives the justice of the way by which we are absolved and leads up our peace of heart into full assurance of faith.

One can speak of an immature assurance based on Christ's work in the believer and the need to labour for a fuller assurance of faith that should be the normal accompaniment of a work of grace. It is found in looking to the finished work of Christ. The conscience is now truly assured. 'It can say anything it desires about sin and about grace' says Hallesby. 'Now it can deliver its whole accusation but also proclaim complete absolution.' No assurance can match that.

In one of his hymns, the nineteenth century Evangelical Anglican E. H. Bickersteth raises the question of 'peace, perfect peace, in this dark world of sin?'. He says rightly that it comes because 'the blood of Jesus whispers peace within'. In an earlier hymn, the Strict Baptist William Gadsby wrote

> Peace of conscience, peace with God,
> We obtain through Jesus' blood;
> Jesus' blood speaks solid rest;
> We believe, and we are blest.

6 The Paradise of delight
Developing conscience

So I always take pains to have a clear conscience toward both God and man.   Acts 24:16

'The process of sanctification hones the believer's conscience and keeps it from vanishing.'   John MacArthur

In a collection of sermons entitled *Ouch my conscience* American Baptist pastor and psychology professor Dr W Maurice Hurley wrote that 'the high goal of Christian faith is that men should have developed within them a mature conscience'.

Is he right? Once a person is awakened and converted, does he have any further use for his conscience?

The Law

There are those who deny that the law has any significant place in the Christian life. They would not accept the term but they are often referred to as antinomian, that is those who are 'against the law'. The texts that supposedly support their views, are well known (see John 1:17, Romans 6:14, 7:4, 10:4, Ephesians 2:15). The germ of truth in what they say is that no man can be saved by the law (Romans 3:21–22; 4:5; 8:3, etc.). Nevertheless, the law continues to be important to the Christian as a revelation of God's will.

Thus the renewed conscience of the Christian is a most important ally, for there lies both the moral record containing God's law and the means of applying it. Previously an enemy, the conscience now becomes a friend. It not only keeps the believer alive to a proper sense of sin but also preserves him from self-deception by helping him to probe deep into his inner life before God.

By holding before believers the ideal of perfection etched on the moral record the conscience performs not only the negative task of denouncing but also the positive one of urging on to better works. Eschewing the twin dangers of sheer legalism and practical antinomianism, the believer who heeds his renewed and enlightened conscience will follow the way of faith, believing in 'the requirements of God, even though they are impossible'.

Hallesby says, the conscience 'does not give up the requirement of perfection even though it sees its own imperfect fulfilment of the law each day'. Once again we are reminded of the importance of preaching the law—this time to believers as well as to unbelievers.

This truth comes out in Bunyan's own inimitable style in *The Holy War*. Following the recapture of *Mansoul* by Shaddai there are a number of changes. Mr Conscience, previously Town Recorder, no longer has his old job. That work now passes to Mr Knowledge. This is a little clumsy but is intended to stress that the believer now has the truth in his heart. Mr Conscience becomes Town Preacher. He is subordinate to the Lord Secretary (the Holy Spirit) to whom he must go for information and knowledge about all 'high and supernatural things'. Because of his age and feebleness, he also needs frequent drafts of Christ's blood. The converted conscience, in other words, stands in need of the work of the Spirit and of fortification by the atonement of Christ.

A little later Bunyan describes a time of declension in Mansoul. An awakening comes partly through a powerful and authoritative sermon from Mr Conscience, a sermon designed to convict the people of their sins afresh.

> The people, when sermon was done, were scarce able to go to their homes or to betake themselves to their employs the week after, they were so sermon-smitten and also so sermon-sick by being smitten that they knew not what to do.

Mr Conscience bewailed not only the sins of Mansoul but his own failures too. Bunyan is describing a dramatic re-awakening, but whether dramatic or not, the principle remains the same—in the renewed man the renewed conscience continues to accuse and excuse. He now also has a properly informed moral record, the aid of the Holy Spirit and the sweet realisation that Christ's blood cleanses from all unrighteousness.

A good conscience

The New Testament often speaks of the believer as having a good or a clear conscience, as noted, and it has a high regard for such a blessing. Some would distinguish between a good conscience, a clear conscience and a conscience void of offence, as if these were degrees of excellence. There are certainly degrees in the purity of the conscience but it is unlikely that we are to detect three stages of development from the statements in Acts 23:1 ('I have lived my life before God in all good conscience up to this day') 2 Timothy 1:3 ('I thank God whom I serve, as did my ancestors, with a clear conscience, as I remember you') and Acts 24:16 ('So I always take pains to have a clear conscience toward both God and man').

On several occasions Paul says he has a good conscience or something similar. There are also references to this elsewhere in the New Testament. In these references we see that a good or clear conscience is necessary in a number of areas.

- *Sincerity.* As an aid to scrupulous honesty and sincerity. This is exemplified in Paul himself. In Romans 9:1 he speaks of his conscience bearing witness to his honesty 'in the Holy Spirit' (in *Holy War* terms, the Lord Secretary and his subordinate preacher agree). In 2 Corinthians 1:12, his conscience testified, 'that we behaved in the world with simplicity and godly sincerity, not by earthly wisdom but by the grace of God, and supremely so toward you.' Despite the Corinthians' accusations, Paul's conscience was clear.

- *Love.* As one of the sources of true Christian love (along with a pure heart and a sincere faith). See 1 Timothy 1:5 ('... love, that issues from a pure heart and a good conscience and a sincere faith.')

- *Faithfulness.* As a means of remaining faithful. One needs both faith and a good conscience for this. See 1 Timothy 1:19.

- *Maturity.* As a help to holding the deep truths of the faith. A distinguishing mark of the New Testament deacon was a good conscience—in order to do this, according to 1 Timothy 3:9.

- *Duty.* As a help to doing one's duty and remaining faithful. This comes out in Acts 23:1 and 2 Timothy 1:3, as quoted above.

- *Worthiness.* As a way of being worthy of the prayers of God's people. This is the implication of what is said in Hebrews 13:18. It is hypocritical to ask God's people to pray for you and then not strive to keep a good conscience.

- *Bearing witness.* As a help to maintaining a faithful witness to the unbeliever. A good conscience is important for this. In 1 Peter 3:16 we read about 'having a good conscience, so that, when you are slandered, those who revile your good behaviour in Christ may be put to shame.' (1 Peter 3:16).

- *Prayer.* As a help to our own prayers. It is necessary to have a clear conscience (a heart that does not condemn) for our prayers to be heard. See 1 John 3:21–22.

A good conscience is vital for holy Christian living. Not for one moment should anyone doubt the high value placed on such a thing by the New Testament. As Augustine is said to have enthused, 'a good conscience is the palace of Christ, the temple of the Holy Spirit, the paradise of delight, the standing Sabbath of the saints'. Or as the nineteenth century American theologian William S Plumer put it 'a good conscience is the best treasure ever held, the best pleasure ever tasted, the best honour ever conferred.'

The duty of the Christian is surely clear, therefore. He has a duty to keep his conscience informed by God's Word. He must do nothing to grieve the Holy Spirit, the Lord of conscience. He must keep looking to the cross of the Lord Jesus Christ so that his heart or conscience may know peace. Further, it is clear that he must never go against his conscience. This subordinate preacher is there, like all good preachers, to keep him in line with God's Word. This preacher, like Grimshaw of Haworth was apocryphally said to have done, may even subject his faculties to 'whips and chastisements, if they shall not willingly hearken to do (God's) commandments.'

Obeying conscience

It is important for us to be clear as to just what a good conscience is. A good conscience is one that is not only biblically informed but that is also obeyed. What it says, the believer does and where there is any failure to do so there is immediate repentance. While this attitude persists, the conscience will not become blunted or benumbed. In Acts 24:16 Paul says that he *takes pains* always to keep his conscience clear before men and God. He strives for it. It is his constant exercise.

Paul did not attempt to ignore his conscience until it had to preach a hell-fire sermon at him. He worked hard to keep it clear all the time. Sadly, David Fountain's words of some years ago, are still true today,

> It can safely be said that the majority of evangelical consciences are lazy. It requires effort to exercise the conscience and this is unpleasant to the flesh.

Exercising the conscience and keeping it healthy is certainly no easy task but, as Jean Antoine Petit-Senn observed, 'a good conscience never costs as much as it is worth'. It is said that 'the cost of peace is eternal vigilance'. It is the same with a clear conscience—the price is eternal vigilance.

The perfected or cleansed conscience leads to a good conscience. The good conscience is the inevitable accompaniment of a pure heart (one renewed by the Holy Spirit) and a sincere faith (in Christ's atoning work) as is clear from 1 Timothy 1:5.

New Testament baptism was administered at the start of the Christian life. Its importance lay not in 'removal of dirt from the body' but 'the pledge of a clear conscience toward God' (1 Peter 3:21, NIV). A good conscience, in the double sense of being clear (not accusing) and functioning accurately, is the gift of every child of God. The conscience functions accurately because it has been renewed in every part and it is clear because of the blood of Christ. It is impossible for conscience to discover such things by itself. John Owen points out that 'it is by a principle of Gospel light alone that is directed to condemn all sin and yet to acquit all sinners that are purged' (i.e. cleansed).

The preacher and hymn writer John Newton once wrote,

> I saw one hanging on a tree
> In agony and blood
> Who fixed his languid eye on me
> As near the cross I stood.
>
> My conscience felt and owned my guilt
> And plunged me in despair.
> I saw my sins his blood had spilt
> And helped to nail him there.

But then, having recognised his sin, he notes of Christ,

> A second look he gave, which said,
> 'I freely all forgive'
> This blood if for thy ransom paid;
> I die that thou may'st live.
>
> Thus while his death my sin displays
> In all its blackest hue
> Such is the mystery of grace
> It seals my pardon too.

This is what the good conscience experiences. The conscience becomes good through faith in Christ and his atonement. Calvin wrote similarly

> If we ask in what way the conscience can be made quiet before God, we shall find the only way to be that unmerited righteousness be conferred upon us as a gift of God.

Wherever the conscience convicts there must be confession and genuine repentance. Meanwhile, we must submit to God's Word, giving heed to preaching or meditation on its message and always applying what we find to the conscience. Hallesby says

> The development of conscience is therefore conditional fundamentally upon the believer living himself into the Word of

God, particularly that part of the Word that deals with the will of God.

The first thing to be applied to the conscience from the Word is the fact of justification by faith. The second is the reality of Christian freedom. Ridderbos has commented,

> The liberty given in Christ is mirrored in the conscience not as liberty from moral decision, but as freedom from guilt before God.

In other words, because of justification the believer is free to live for God. Along with this knowledge, the Christian stands in need of wisdom in order to know how properly to apply God's Word. Those who lack wisdom are urged, in James 1, to ask God for it. Solomon is a great example to us of such asking and his Proverbs will be a great help too, although it is salutary to remember that he too fell.

A clear conscience

To have a clear conscience is not to be sinless. A clear conscience is not the same as a silent conscience. A conscience can only be kept clear provided that we allow it to speak and if we acknowledge that it speaks truthfully. We must then repent from the sins that it uncovers, seeking, by God's grace, not to fall into those sins again. Hallesby adds

> Another sign of a pure conscience is to acknowledge the truth of its accusations and not only accept but seek the reckoning!

For this reason the person who has a clear conscience will be a person who is often in prayer and who also takes time to subject himself to regular self-examination. Such a person is concerned about his actions, his words, his thoughts, his motives. He is on the look out for anything false that is beginning to permeate his life.

Hurley points out that 'the mature conscience is a constantly growing one'. This growth is chiefly in its becoming ever more tender. Baird compares it to a beautiful tender plant. By careful cultivation the grace of form and the richness of the fragrance are developed. A conscience must not become over-sensitive but it must be tender.

It must be sensitive about the essential issues and not merely secondary ones, inward matters not merely outward ones. Slowly but surely, if rightly guided, the conscience matures. As Hebrews 5:14 puts it, it is trained by constant use 'to distinguish good from evil'. The Christian who has such a conscience is serious minded and circumspect. He avoids temptation where he can. He may well be accused of narrow-mindedness, even by his fellow believers. Matthew Henry counsels, 'if we take care to keep a good conscience we may leave it to God to take care of our good name.'

Besides, such people are done with the burden of a bad conscience. Regardless of the cost involved, they have no wish to return to the old unrest. How we need such people today! They are solid, conscientious, dependable and honest. Further, they are

Straightforward. 'Inconsistency of life is utterly destructive of peace of conscience. The two things are incompatible. They cannot and they will not go together.' (J. C. Ryle). The best Christians know this and avoid double-mindedness.

Dignified. 'Dignity is the reward of holding oneself accountable to *conscience*.' (Wes Fessler).

Confident. 'A good conscience and a good confidence go together' (Thomas Brooks).

Joyful. 'We can do nothing well without joy and a good conscience which is the ground of joy' (Richard Sibbes)

Brave. 'Once a person is gripped by the voice of conscience a power is harnessed by which acts of heroic courage may issue forth. A conscience captured by the Word of God is both noble and powerful' (R. C. Sproul)

How rare such people are in days of spiritual dearth. There are plenty of hard-working, keen, enthusiastic believers about today perhaps but their consciences often seem to be relatively insensitive. They are careless. They are easily compromised. They give in to temptation too easily or they are in the grip of some life dominating sin. Such people are easy prey for Satan who goes around like a roaring lion looking for someone to devour (1 Peter 5:8).

A sensitive conscience is a great bulwark against such things especially when they, as Hallesby puts it,

> have become a natural part of the soul's hidden life in God. It has become part of love's very union with God and preserves it as a holy union.

The sensitive conscience, of course, speaks with great authority. The more our wills submit to our consciences, the stronger conscience becomes. Having trained many years ago as a school teacher, it has struck me that some teachers with authority can control a class of 30 or 40 children, even though those same children are usually misbehaved with others. Teachers unable to maintain discipline are faced with an ever worsening situation as the children egg each other on to ever greater extremes of bad behaviour. In a similar way, a sensitive conscience spares the believer from many of the daily struggles faced by those whose consciences are less sensitive.

Sanctification and conscience

The conscience is essential in the ongoing work of sanctification in the life of the believer. Drawing on Hallesby, Robert Solomon identifies six things that conscience does for the believer, four negative or preventative and two positive or enabling. Conscience acts as

1. A guard against self-deception

To quote Jeremiah 17:9 yet again 'the heart is deceitful above all things, and desperately sick' and is not easy to understand. Because salvation is by grace, even the heart of flesh may be tempted to try and take advantage of grace and cheapen it. A false sense of security can give us the idea that sin does not matter and we can easily become lax. Thankfully, the conscience of a converted sinner will keep him from deception by reminding him that God calls the believer to holiness.

2. An upholder of the perfect standard

Whereas before conversion a person's moral record may have been rather deficient, after conversion constant study of the Bible means that the conscience will bring the whole outward as well as the inner life of the believer into the light of the Word of God and point out even the minutest infractions of God's holy and loving will in deed, word, thought, imagination and desire.

Conscience highlights not only where we are doing what is wrong but also where we are failing to do right. It is concerned not only with outward actions but motives too.

3. A force to drive us to Christ

In the converted sinner, conscience will not only point to the high standard of the law but also will point to Christ. Every time we are about to despair, knowing by means of conscience how far short we fall, the converted conscience will also turn us to Christ and the forgiveness for every sin that is found only in him by means of his death on the cross.

4. A cause of pain when there is disobedience
While the joy of sins forgiven is very real, conscience inevitably also causes pain when it reminds us of our many failings. This leads to two very good things—a growing hatred for sin and an increasing longing for heaven.

5. A means of fulfilling the law
Although we need to know what is revealed in God's Word and the work of the Holy Spirit within, if we are to keep God's law as we should, the conscience is also essential in enabling us to live as we ought, especially in the work of reminding us of what God requires.

6. A means of doing the will of God
Obedience to God's will is essential to living the Christian life. Again, the conscience is vital if we are going to be obedient, helping us to be clear what God's will is and encouraging us to do it.

Deep groaning and conscience
There are a large number of man made proverbs extolling the good conscience as a soft pillow, a continual feast, a coat of mail or a continual Christmas!

On the other hand, as we have noted, a sensitive conscience inevitably leads to what Hallesby calls

> the deep groaning in the soul of the believer ... a chronic pain

which increases rather than diminishes in intensity ... not a symptom of illness ... on the contrary a sign of health.

As Henry Twells wrote, 'They who fain would serve thee best are conscious most of wrong within'. Paul's increasing sense of sin has often been remarked upon. In 1 Corinthians 15:9 he says 'For I am the least of the apostles, unworthy to be called an apostle ...' Some while later, in Ephesians 3:8, he speaks of himself as 'the very least of all the saints'. Near the end of his life, in 1 Timothy 1:15–16, he is simply the chief of sinners. Paradoxically, the more holy a person grows the more conscious they become of how sinful they are.

Despite the inevitable tension, the conscientious Christian feels the need continually to consult his conscience. He will not violate it for any reason. He seeks to subject his whole life, little by little, to the dictates of God's Word. His *raison d'être* centres on Colossians 3:17 and 1 Corinthians 10:31. Whatever he does, whether in word or deed, he does it all in the name of the Lord Jesus, giving thanks to God the Father through him. Even if only eating or drinking, whatever he does, he does it all for the glory of God.

Finally, following Hallesby again, we notice three characteristics of the rightly sensitive conscience.

It will impel us, firstly, to seek the cross of Christ. Secondly, it will enhance our desire for fellowship with the Lord and an ever more intimate relationship will be established. Finally, this will lead to an increasing sense of the peace of God, the 'peace like a river' of Isaiah 66:12, a peace that transcends understanding. We can use the words of Isaac Watts to pray

> Order my footsteps by thy Word
> And make my heart sincere;
> Let sin have no dominion, Lord,
> But keep my conscience clear.

7 Seared with a hot iron
Degenerating conscience

Now the Spirit expressly says that in later times some will depart from the faith by devoting themselves to deceitful spirits and teachings of demons, through the insincerity of liars whose consciences are seared,
1 Timothy 4:1–2

'… though wicked men cannot quite stifle their consciences, yet their consciences do but, as it were, talk in their sleep, and they take no more notice of them, than they do of their dreams'
Samuel Annesley

We have said something about the conscience in the unawakened, awakened and converted sinner. Next we want to consider some of the aberrations and deficiencies of conscience that occur in believers and in unbelievers.

One of the difficulties we face when we come to this part of the subject is that a variety of terms have been used to describe these abnormalities and inadequacies. This variety is not confined to theologians and different Bible translations but is something that is characteristic of the Bible itself. Having said that, it is fair to say that when it comes to those who are believers, the main term used in the Bible for deficiencies of conscience is the word *weak*. The weak conscience is dealt with chiefly in 1 Corinthians 8–10. In this category we can include an over-sensitive or over-scrupulous conscience, an immature one, a doubting one and, perhaps, one that is perverted. The danger facing such a conscience is that it should be emboldened, wounded or defiled. We will look at the weak conscience later. In this chapter we focus on the conscience of the unbeliever; its deadness, decay and other deficiencies.

Deficiencies

In discussing an evil conscience, Puritan writers often made careful distinctions. Ephraim Huit, for example, wrote of four degrees of evil, going from laziness and contentment with natural light through to conformity to sin and Satan's image, hating truth and loving evil. Between these comes wilful and affected ignorance where, like elephants, men muddy the water to avoid their reflections and, like owls, shun the light of law preaching and give up the struggle against sin, willingly giving in to temptation.

Still

More common is the distinction between a still, quiet (or dead) conscience and a *stirring, unquiet* evil one. This *still* conscience is not completely still but it is very weak. Richard Bernard likens it to 'a dumb minister in a Parish' that is one who will not speak out to bring reformation to his church but lets the people quietly go on to destruction. Jeremiah Dyke uses a similar picture, when writing of an *ignorant* conscience, which he calls 'toothless and tongueless' and blind. It is caused by ignorance, conceit, pride, respectability or negligence of what might rightly stir it. It is found in 'all dull Nabals and the muddy spirited' and many who are outwardly respectable and wise in their own eyes. The evil in it is the failure of conscience to function. William Fenner appears to be thinking of a still, evil conscience when he writes of an *unfaithful* one. It is typically silent, large (or broad) and remiss. Such a state of affairs arises from ignorance or from slighting conscience. Some are even violent against it or stop its mouth.

Some go into more detail than others in delineating this *still* conscience. Richard Bernard is very thorough and discovers as many as nine subdivisions. These are

- Dead. He reserves the term *dead* for the sort found in infants, the insane and all so entirely sunk in sin that they are past feeling remorse.

- Blind. He applies the word *blind* to pagans and those who, sometimes despite a Christian background, are in gross ignorance. Some are unsighted or *stone-blind*, others partially sighted or *purblind*, being sensitive about some major things but having only the most general idea of Christian things.

- Sleepy. Even a good man's conscience may sometimes sleep but by a *sleepy* conscience is meant a habitually drowsy one. It soon stops working, is difficult to rouse, works rather weakly and soon gives in and goes to sleep again. It only works if it constantly hears threats. It is the result of coldness, neglect and worldliness. For Fenner it is 'very dangerous' as it allows a person to see his faults without ever putting them right. It does not cause a man to feel the burden of his sins, so he never comes to Christ. Some writers prefer to call this a *benumbed* conscience. Ames says it is dull in pricking to good and accusing of evil. Perkins says it is like a sleeping wild beast—tame enough in slumber but ferocious if roused. When sickness or death come, it is awoken by God's hand, begins to stand on its hind legs and shows its fierce eyes, ready to rip out the throat of the soul. Dyke uses a similar image for what he calls a *secure* conscience. He distinguishes between a truce and true peace. The truce of a falsely secure conscience cannot last.

- Secure. By a *secure* conscience Bernard, on the other hand, in his fourth category, means a falsely secure one, one worse than sleepy in that it occupies the mind with gathering arguments to counter conscience. He likens such people to the rich man in Jesus' parable who tells himself to eat, drink and be merry. Such people have false views of God's mercy, low views of holiness and unrealistic ideas of deathbed repentance.

- Lukewarm. Even in seventeenth century England some, familiar with various shades of Christianity and world religions, remained impartial to them all, believing that all roads lead to God. The result of this is what Bernard calls a *lukewarm* conscience.

- Large. Similar in some ways is a *large* conscience, the sixth category. This refers to a man who 'can swallow down sins great and many; that can admit cart-loads thereof without any rub or let' to his conscience. The only sin here is being found out.

- Spandex. Bernard, following Richard Greenham before him, warns against making conscience 'like a cheveril purse' and stretching it too far or too narrow'. The word *cheveril,* which refers to stretchable leather, like kid's leather, was used for making gloves or purses. Perhaps a *spandex conscience* would be the modern term. We are referring to those who pick and choose what to be conscientious about. Such people make conscience subject to their own wills, or are hypocritical or deceitful.

- A *benumbed* conscience, Bernard's eighth category, is often caused by lack of repentance and can affect a believer—David, before Nathan confronted him about his sin with Bathsheba, is an obvious example. Fenner likens a benumbed state to deep sleep.

Degeneration

In the unbeliever, the evil or guilty conscience can lead to the corrupted conscience and even the rejected or seared conscience (Bernard's ninth category). These dangers, of course, are not confined to rank unbelievers but are possibilities too for professing Christians.

What we have already said about the conscience in the unbeliever has underlined the fact that the natural conscience is always deficient. Due to the fall of man, the knowledge of the law of God found in the moral record is incomplete; the conscience itself never performs its work efficiently and even if it did, the mind is so darkened by nature that there is often a resolute refusal to comply with conscience's demands. Conscience is bad, not in the sense that it always makes the person feel bad but in the sense that it does not and cannot function as it ought. The conscience of fallen man needs to be cleansed from 'dead works' (Hebrews 6:1) in order that he may serve the Living God. Until that guilty conscience is cleansed, the ultimate sense of deserving God's judgement can never be legitimately erased.

Clearly the level and type of guilt on a conscience will vary from person to person. The New Testament reveals that on the day of judgement one of the factors that will be taken into account is the measure of light on the truth the conscience has received (see Luke 12:47–48). Further, that knowledge, however great or little, can be resisted or neglected to varying degrees. Now if a man continues to sin against the light and resist his conscience it can become seriously damaged. David Fountain speaks of those who, 'though cut to the heart by the truth of God ... resist the gracious influences of the Spirit ...' He refers us for this to Acts 7:54 and the fury and gnashing of teeth in response to Stephen's sermon.

Some decide the best thing,

> ... is to do a deal with it in order to placate it. They are like Herod who, being convicted of sin as a result of John's ministry ... *did many things and heard him gladly* (Mark 6:20). They may go to many lengths, and be subject to much conflict, as was the case with Pilate who sought earnestly Christ's acquittal.

Eventually, however, such people, like Pilate, get to the point where they wish to wash their hands of conscience. Conscience is defiled and disoriented. The desire to jettison it is strong.

It is never possible to be completely free of your conscience. Nevertheless, it can become so calloused, so deadened, that it hardly functions. We can understand people saying of someone 'he has no conscience'. The most extreme example of this would be the criminal psychopath. Some suggest that this is due to genetic factors but Dr Gaius Davies, in a book on the subject of stress, suggests that poor teaching and neglect are more likely factors. We do not rule out psychological factors in some cases. This condition has its counterpart in the religious world firstly in the shape of the total apostate but also with the hypocritical and legalistic Pharisee. At times apostasy and hypocrisy walk hand in hand. There is a link between the evil conscience and the accusing conscience and the insensitive conscience. As David Fountain, again, points out,

> The person who has an evil conscience invariably has an insensitive conscience at the same time ... He wants to make his own conscience a guide for other people.

Data in the New Testament

In three places, all in Paul's pastoral letters, this lowest condition is spoken of.

Firstly, in 1 Timothy 1:19, speaking of the need for Timothy to hold on to faith and a good conscience, Paul says 'By rejecting this, some have made shipwreck of their faith'. William Hendriksen puts it helpfully, 'they have thrown away the rudder conscience and shipwreck is inevitable'.

Then, in 1 Timothy 4:2, we read of insincere or hypocritical liars who have abandoned the faith. Their 'consciences are seared' ('as with a hot iron' the NIV suggests). The image here is of the branding or cauterisation of human flesh which results in desensitisation. Today surgeons will sometimes cauterise flesh in order to remove tissue or stop bleeding. Such flesh is rendered useless. Or to use an image suggested by Dyke, conscience becomes 'like Galley slaves backs, so bebrawned over with often lashing, that an ordinary lash will not make them so much as once shuck in their shoulders.' That such people are not only apostate but Pharisaical too comes out in verse 3 (they 'forbid marriage and require abstinence from foods that God created to be received with thanksgiving').

Thirdly, in Titus 1:15, we read of people whose minds and consciences are defiled or corrupted. The word Paul uses means to stain or pollute, to contaminate. He is referring not just to any unbeliever but to those who claim to know God and yet deny it by their actions.

Some have sought to differentiate in these three cases. No doubt it could be demonstrated that Paul has different people in mind in each case, nevertheless in all three places he is clearly dealing with the same species of sin. Whether we say a man has rejected his conscience, cauterised it or simply corrupted it, we cannot deny that it is possible to so harden or deaden or corrupt the conscience that it ceases to function in any significant way. However, before that dreadful point is reached a man has to travel a sometimes long road of increasing hardness.

Downward path

The important question for us to answer here is how and why the conscience becomes deranged and ineffectual. Only if we know that can we take steps to counteract the danger. Back in Romans

2:14–15 we noticed that it was a man's thoughts or opinions, his will, that accused or excused on the basis of the witness of the conscience proper. When the will takes notice of conscience's witness, the conscience can develop and grow strong. Hallesby compares it to the use of ones lungs. As a general rule, the more you inhale and exhale, the stronger your lungs become. So with the conscience. The more often the conscience is disobeyed the less categorical are its demands.

Think of the pit ponies once used in South Wales and elsewhere in the coal mining industry. They were underground in the darkness so long that they often became blind. In a similar way, the darkness of sin destroys conscience's faculty of sight. Robert Solomon quotes a Native American in Canada cited by J Oswald Sanders. He said of conscience

> It is a three-cornered thing inside me that stands still when I am good. When I do wrong, it turns round and hurts me very much. But if I keep on doing wrong it will turn so much that the corners become worn out and it does not hurt any more.

John King warned, *'in giving way to temptation, we cannot* possibly avoid the inflicting of deep injury on our conscience'. Sixteenth century theologian and mathematician Isaac Barrow described the process in this way,

> Conscience is a check to beginners in sin, reclaiming them from it and rating them for it; but this in longstanders becometh useless;

either failing to discharge its office, or assaying it to no purpose: having often been slighted, it will be weary of chiding; or, if it be not wholly dumb, we shall be deaf to its reproof: as those who live by cataracts or downfalls of water, are, by continual noise, so deafened as not to hear or mind it.

Sadly, this can be verified from experience. To go against your conscience for the first time and commit a particular sin can be most painful. There is a great struggle beforehand and strong recriminations afterwards. The second time, the struggle is not so great, the recriminations are lighter. Very soon a bad habit is formed and, except maybe at random moments, there is scarcely a murmur from the unawakened conscience. When this happens in several areas of life, conscience and the will become estranged. As one writer has pointed out, a major reason why some people refuse to listen to their consciences is because they will not take advice from a total stranger!

Interestingly, there is also evidence for this from the desensitisation of children exposed to long periods of watching television. In a book called *The Evil Eye* Guy Lyon Playfair describes the work of H J. Eysenck in this area,

> Now, said Eysenck, how would we go about destroying someone's conscience if we wanted to? His answer: ... by a process of deconditioning. Viewing television in the home offered ideal surroundings for the process. Scenes of second hand violence are shown while viewers are comfortable and relaxed.

Without necessarily accepting all the tenets of behavioural science, we can see just how the conscience could be desensitised in this way.

Defining traits

But how can a person know if his or her conscience is becoming hardened? In his little book on conscience, Warren Wiersbe has a chapter entitled *A failure to be serious about sin*. There he lists five defining traits of the man who is on this downward trail.

- Playing with sin. Those who are not serious about sin are constantly in danger of alienating their conscience, which is always serious about sin. Playing with sin is like playing with fire.

- Shallow confession and repentance. It is possible to delude oneself that ones conscience is healthy because of faithfulness in formal confession and repentance. However, if this is only a superficial act, it will do more harm than good. Church father Clement of Alexandria warned that *'Repeatedly asking for pardon* for frequent trespasses is not repentance but only the appearance of repentance'.

- Measuring sin. G Campbell Morgan used to speak of 'sins in good standing'. This is another form of superficiality. 'He has limited its activities to a small area of external observances and petty taboos'. One writer speaks about calipers, which he describes as a handy tool for measuring distance across odd-shaped items. As he says, *people in many professions use calipers to take critical measurements.* They can provide high levels of precision and are especially useful in measuring odd-shaped items that cannot be measured with a standard measuring tool. He then says

> *Sin is one of those odd shaped* things. It takes all sorts of forms and as humans, we love to measure sin … especially in other folks. *God, however, does not take such measurements.* Sin is sin! The smallest in our estimation is enough to destroy fellowship. The largest can bring us to think it unforgivable.

- Concern about reputation. As with the previous category, here we meet the Pharisee once again. 'They are taken up with the impression they make on others'.

- Arguing with truth. Such a person is increasingly anxious to justify himself.

David Fountain rightly seizes on the word *superficiality* to sum it all up. We can, perhaps, understand this adolescence in young Christians but those who do not grow up spiritually become a danger to themselves and to others.

Distraction methods

People attempt to cope with the hardening of conscience in different ways. As we have suggested, the Pharisee surrounds himself with a heap of good deeds to be done, rules to be kept, conscientiousness to be maintained over the minutiae of life. The things that really matter are overlooked. It was for this very failure that the Lord upbraided the Pharisees of his day. See Matthew 23, especially verse 23 where Jesus says

> Woe to you, scribes and Pharisees, hypocrites! For you tithe mint and dill and cumin, and have neglected the weightier matters of the law: justice and mercy and faithfulness. These you ought to have done, without neglecting the others.

Think, for example, how the Pharisees could show great scrupulosity about not entering Pilate's house at Passover, while at the same time they were seeking the death of an innocent man. Saul is an Old Testament example of the same sort of thing. See 1 Samuel 15:30 where he is concerned chiefly about his reputation. It is seen again in 1 Samuel 28 and 31.

In other cases, people turn to drink in order to drown their protesting consciences. Some use other drugs or find ways of escaping into a fantasy world of make-believe. Others bury themselves in their work or a ceaseless round of activity. None of these expedients will do anything to solve the real problem.

Deliverance?

Is there any way back for the person whose conscience has become so hardened? The Bible certainly gives us hope. It is not an easy thing to deaden the conscience completely. There is hope, even for a man like Saul of Tarsus. In 1 Timothy 1:13 and 14 he explains that 'though formerly' he 'was a blasphemer, persecutor, and insolent opponent' he says

> I received mercy because I had acted ignorantly in unbelief, and the grace of our Lord overflowed for me with the faith and love that are in Christ Jesus.

Many believers were understandably sceptical when they first heard the report that 'he who used to persecute us is now preaching the faith he once tried to destroy' (Galatians 1:23; Acts 9:26). Nevertheless it was true—where sin had once abounded, grace now abounded much more.

This example and others like it should warn us not to be too quick to write off a man's conscience as seared, thrown overboard or so corrupted that it is beyond the pale. Paul's descriptions of the unbelieving heart, for example in Ephesians 2:1–3 and 4:17–19, sound as though there can be no remedy yet the verses that follow in Ephesians 2:4–10 and from 4:20 show that is not always the case. In Augustus Toplady's biblically informed terms 'the things impossible to men are possible to God'.

Fenner gets it about right when he says 'such may come to repent but it is a thousand to one if ever they do.' Repentance can only be by an extraordinary work of God.

Done deal?

On the other hand, we must recognise that the Bible speaks about the unforgivable sin (Matthew 12:31), a sin that leads to death (1 John 5:16) and an irretrievable hardening of the heart (Hebrews 3:13, 15). The work of the Holy Spirit is to convict or awaken the sinner. This, we have seen, is a work done in the conscience.

However, when one's conscience has been burned out, how is conviction of sin possible? The conscience can lose the spiritual faculty of receiving and possessing a conviction. The barometer no longer functions; the watchdog cannot bark; the sense of taste is gone; the umpire has been driven out and anarchy means the game cannot be played.

There is an unseen line over which a man may step, a point of no return. From that unknown moment on, he is utterly without hope. That line is not crossed by committing one single sin, no matter how wicked it may be. Rather, as with certain heart diseases, it is the slow but sure clogging of the arteries, as it were, that leads ultimately to death.

Says Hallesby

> That organ in man which constitutes the point of contact for God's salvation has been wasted and destroyed. Man's last possibility of being saved has thus been lost, because sorrow for sin has become an impossibility ... God cannot create a new conscience in man if he deliberately and wilfully destroys his powers of conscience.

It is as if a gravestone stands over conscience until God wakes it at the judgement when the books, including the book of conscience, will be opened.

Like Judas Iscariot, such a man is capable of great remorse. Hebrews 10:26–27 remind us of the fearful expectations of the apostate,

> For if we go on sinning deliberately after receiving the knowledge of the truth, there no longer remains a sacrifice for sins, but a fearful expectation of judgement, and a fury of fire that will consume the adversaries.

In some mysterious way the terrors of conscience remain, while the motivation to do what is right has gone. Perhaps this is what the nineteenth century Bishop of Calcutta, Daniel Wilson, had in mind when he said that if we fail to listen to conscience's whispers we will have to listen to its thunders. It is a fearful state to come to. The only way to avoid it is to give conscience its proper place.

Danger

Hallesby warns that

> The most fearful power which man possesses is that he by his will can destroy the very humanity which is within himself and thus make of himself not an animal but a devil.

How does such a thing happen? By deliberately continuing to sin, despite having received a knowledge of the truth. That is all that it takes to destroy God's precious gift of the conscience. Therefore, for the professing Christian to leave one sin unconfessed, one sin unrepented of; to persist for one moment against the dictates of conscience, is to live most dangerously indeed.

As for the unbeliever, he must be urged to start listening to his conscience again. It needs to be transformed, quickened to spiritual life. To slightly update some words of the late nineteenth-century preacher J.H. Jowett, who lived in the days of chloroform, 'Let us vigilantly resist all teaching that would anaesthetise our consciences'.

8 Fully persuaded
Weaknesses in conscience

... Each one should be fully convinced in his own mind.
Romans 14:5

'Ironically, a weak conscience is more likely to accuse than a strong conscience' John MacArthur

We come next to the subject of the weak conscience. In practice, this is an affliction confined to believers. Weakness in conscience can lead a person to have an emboldened, a defiled or a wounded conscience. These are the terms Paul uses in 1 Corinthians 8, one of two places where he deals with the matter of the weak conscience. He also deals with the weak conscience in Romans 14 and 15. One of Paul's aims in his earlier letter is to show the Corinthians the limitations of knowledge, including the self-knowledge that conscience provides. This was something they had not really appreciated in the past.

The subject that prompts Paul to write as he does in 1 Corinthians 8 and which he continues with in Chapter 9 more broadly and returns to and concludes in Chapter 10, is the matter of food sacrificed to idols. In the pagan city of Corinth it was common for meat to be offered to idols before being sold in the market place. You never quite knew when this had happened and when it had not. For some of the Corinthian believers this raised the question of whether it was right to eat meat that appeared to have been or that had been offered in this way.

As far as many were concerned, perhaps Jews and former Jewish proselytes in particular, it was not really an issue. In reality, idols are nothing at all so the fact someone thinks he has offered meat to a god that does not exist should not bother the conscience of a Christian one bit. Others, however, perhaps Gentiles with a pagan background in particular, were concerned about what was happening. For them it was against their conscience to eat such meat. In this case simply to say 'do what is right' and 'follow your conscience' was not enough. Because people's minds and consciences were telling them different things, it was becoming another source of contention and potential division in a church already prone to fragmentation.

Strong and weak

It is in the course of dealing with this issue that Paul refers to *the strong* and the *weak brother* or the one with a *weak conscience*. As we have suggested, *the strong* are most likely to be Jewish believers and *the weak* Gentiles with a pagan background. The term *strong* is not necessarily entirely complimentary and the term *weak* is not necessarily entirely pejorative.

The weak Christians in this case are those who (8:7) 'through former association with idols, eat food as really offered to an idol, and their conscience, being weak, is defiled.'

Paul is clear that such an opinion is deficient. To think like that is a mark of immaturity.

Therefore, as to the eating of food offered to idols, we know that 'an idol has no real existence,' and that 'there is no God but one.' For although there may be so-called gods in heaven or on earth— as indeed there are many 'gods' and many 'lords'- yet for us there is one God, the Father, from whom are all things and for whom we exist, and one Lord, Jesus Christ, through whom are all things and through whom we exist. ... Food will not commend us to God. We are no worse off if we do not eat, and no better off if we do. (1 Corinthians 8:4-6, 8)

Paul does not defend the point of view of the weak from the plain facts but he does defend the person of the weak from the tyranny of the strong. His opening remark is to the effect that love is far more important than knowledge. It is not enough simply to be strong, in the sense of knowing, rather than weak, in the sense of being ignorant. Rather, love is the paramount thing.

There is some debate as to what exactly constitutes the weakness of the weak conscience here. Clearly, the weakness in mind springs from the fact that this person is liable to be wounded or defiled, probably by being emboldened to go against his conscience. C. A. Pierce, referring back to Luke 17:1 and the verses that follow, quotes L. S. Thornton. In a collected essay on Apostolic Ministry edited by Kenneth Kirk, he identifies the weak with the *little ones* of whom Jesus speaks and wants to put 'inverted commas' around the word 'weak'. He says it means 'those whom you have the effrontery to despise as weaker brethren'. Pierce points out that the weak conscience is not necessarily the same as the over-sensitive conscience though we can see increased vulnerability in such a person.

It is important to stress that Paul's first concern is to defend the weak against the arrogance of the strong. However, as unhappy as he is with the strong, Paul is not happy for the weak to remain ignorant. It is, in fact, their ignorance that constitutes part of their weakness. The label *weak* may well also point to the fact that these believers were unstable. They had doubting consciences and were easily persuaded to go against them.

Whether a person considers himself to be weak or strong, he faces certain dangers when believers have a difference of conscience. It is all too easy to be encouraged or emboldened (verse 10) to go against conscience because of the example of a stronger brother. This leads to defiling, wounding or even destruction (verses 7, 12 and 11). Of course, it is the person with the over-sensitive conscience who is most likely to face these dangers but wherever conscience is weak, that is uncertain, this danger lurks.

The Dutch theologian G. C. Berkouwer observes

> Paul is here in no way implying the holiness of the consciences of the weak and of each individual—conscience can be related to idolatry!—he is simply concerned to protect the weak from a way of error in connection with something which for them is still a reality and therefore still plays a role in their total relation to God. The motif of Paul's warning is not the unassailability of the conscience, but love toward the weak.

Mahatma Gandhi once said that 'there is a higher court than courts of justice and that is the court of conscience. It supersedes all other courts.' This is not a New Testament understanding of conscience.

Berkouwer agrees with the remark of the Catholic scholar Jacques Dupont that

> the novelty here is not Paul's, but the general Christian message, in which the conscience is not the final norm for conduct, but rather

love, and in love not doing that which one's conscience allows—not as a limitation but as a manifestation of Christian liberty.

The ideal is to have a strong conscience, that is a properly informed one. Believers ought to have strong convictions and ought to know how to exercise their Christian liberty with full peace of conscience, uninfluenced by the mere opinions of others. However, and this is Paul's main concern, if you really are strong, that strength is never to be used to *bully* the weak into submission to your point of view. Here, the Pharisaism that lurks in all of us can so easily raise its ugly head. Not only is it important for the individual adult Christian to act on the guidance of his own conscience rather than that of someone else's conscience but also there is a very real danger of wounding or defiling the weak conscience of a professed brother or sister or even destroying them.

Three categories

In the helpful book *Decision making and the will of God,* which first appeared back in 1980, Garry Friesen, assisted by J Robin Maxson, writes of three categories in connection with differences over conscience—the weaker brother, the convinced brother and the Pharisee. Believers may err to the right or to the left—towards Pharisaism on the one hand or towards weakness on the other.

The weaker brother usually has a sincere belief on a matter but may not be fully convinced about it. He feels that he is in need of teaching rather than being the sort of person who wants to foist his opinions on others. Although at first surprised at the actions of others who differ from him, he is fairly easy to influence and can quickly be encouraged to go against his own conscience and so stumble in his Christian walk.

A 'Pharisee', on the other hand, is at the other end of the spectrum. He is fully convinced of the rightness of his own position and proudly refuses to consider that there might be another view. He wants everyone else to conform to his own viewpoint, even in the case of mature adult Christians who conscientiously disagree with him. He cannot bear the idea of others using their Christian freedom to act in a way that differs in some way from his own. Indeed, he takes offence at such behaviour. If *he* cannot eat it, wear it, listen to it, watch it, read it or use it, then no-one else ought to either!

What all Christians should be aiming at is to be humbly yet confidently persuaded on matters of conscience, while leaving room for making a correction, if they find that should prove necessary. We must recognise that there are differences on many matters among mature believers. Some Christians may object, for example, to wedding rings, mixed bathing, drinking alcohol, wearing or not wearing a tie, women wearing or not wearing hats in church, celebrating Christmas or Easter, addressing God as *you* or *thou*, writing of *him* rather than *Him* or *Yahweh* rather than *Jehovah* when referring to God, to mention just a few examples of the sorts of differences sometimes conscientiously held. We must accept that such differences exist and be willing to discuss such differences in a firm but friendly manner. Such a mature person will not be unduly influenced by the opinions and actions of others. On the one hand, he will avoid causing the weak to stumble and, on the other hand, causing the strong to be needlessly offended.

So, say I believe that it is okay to drink alcohol or to watch feature films and plays in a public place but I know that my fellow believer does not take that view. I do not keep my beliefs secret from him but I do avoid serving him alcohol or inviting him to see the latest film or musical. On the other hand, if I do not drink alcohol or watch feature films and plays in public places, though I may know other Christians who do, I will certainly put forward arguments for my view at appropriate times but I will not presume that because my fellow believer does such things he must be less of a Christian than I am.

Likely candidates

Friesen suggests four groups of people who are the most likely to struggle with a weak conscience and so become vulnerable.

Young adults in the process of leaving the parental nest and beginning to set down their own standards and norms, especially if they have been brought up in a particularly strict or legalistic way.

Young converts, especially those who come from a licentious background that they have had to firmly reject. David Fountain said something similar when he drew an analogy between the awkward period some go through as teenagers and some of the difficulties of being a young Christian. Over-sensitivity in the young Christian is not necessarily a totally bad thing, he argues, but it is a stage that must be left behind at some point.

Those who for one reason or another are unaware of the differences found from culture to culture. You may come from a culture where people always stand for prayer or to read God's Word or where all men wear neck ties to church on Sundays. Do not be offended when you come into contact with good Christians who sit to pray and read the Bible and whose menfolk may not wear a neck tie to church. Back in the 1950s, E. A. Nida gave a striking example of cross-cultural difficulties when he quoted an elder in an Ngbaka church in northern Congo saying 'But we are not going to have our wives dress like prostitutes'. This was in reply to the suggestion made by a missionary that the women should be made to wear blouses to cover their breasts.

Children of believers. Where children have been brought up with one particular set of rules, when they come up against those who have grown up with a different set of rules that seem more attractive, it can be tempting to thoughtlessly kick over the traces and leave behind almost all that has been learned.

Perhaps we can add a fifth category—those who for one reason or another, such as bad training, do not have a properly developed conscience but only one that is weak and immature.

As we have said, the person with the weak conscience is likely to be one who has an over-sensitive conscience. In a celebrated passage in *The Institutes*, dealing with Christian freedom, John Calvin warns against the miseries of an over-sensitive conscience

> The third part of Christian freedom lies in this: regarding outward things that are of themselves 'indifferent', we are not bound before God by any religious obligation preventing us from sometimes using them and at other times not doing so, as it suits us. And the knowledge of this freedom is very necessary to us, for, if it is lacking, our consciences will have no rest and there will be no end of superstitions. ... these matters are more important than is commonly believed. For when consciences once ensnare themselves, they enter a long and inextricable labyrinth, without an easy exit.
>
> If a man begins to doubt whether he may use linen for sheets, shirts, handkerchiefs, and napkins, he will afterwards be uncertain also about hemp; finally, doubt will even arise over tow. For he will turn over in his mind whether he can sup without napkins, or go without a handkerchief. If any man should consider daintier food unlawful, in the end he will not be at peace before God, when he eats either black bread or common victuals, while it occurs to him that he could sustain his body on even coarser foods. If he boggles at sweet wine, he will not with clear conscience drink even flat wine, and finally he will not dare touch water if sweeter and cleaner than other water. To sum up, he will come to the point of considering it wrong to step upon a straw across his path, as the saying goes.

There is some humour here for the outsider but not for the person with the over scrupulous conscience. I well remember as a young Christian getting tangled up over what was right or wrong for a Christian to do on the Lord's Day. It seemed to me that the Sunday newspapers delivered to our unbelieving home were well worth a miss, not only because of their dubious content but also because Sunday was not the day for discovering the 'news of the world'. I was doing well with this until someone pointed out that perhaps I should be just as concerned about Monday's papers which had been prepared and printed on the Lord's Day. The point was made with some humour but it was all lost on me, a boy with a keen conscience who simply wanted to know what was right and wrong. I was only more bewildered and perplexed than I had been before.

When such a condition continues for any length of time, the continual uncertainty and the spiritual conflict can become unbearable. A person can become distraught, almost afraid to speak or act for fear of sin. Thankfully, like me, most young believers grow out of such immaturity but not always and many years of unhappiness and despair can be the result.

Hallesby speaks of a situation where 'essentials and non-essentials become one confused mess'. A person has to speak about the things that are disturbing him to every believer he meets. He draws attention to the way an illness or a physical or mental disability can bring this sort of thing on in an otherwise mature believer. Where there is no apparent cause for it, we are perhaps best to look upon it as a temptation to despair.

What causes the conscience of an otherwise healthy and mature believer to become over-sensitive in this way? The chief problem is usually to do with a pre-occupation with the outward and theoretical side of religion rather than with what is inward and spiritual. This is the problem both with the weaker brother and the Pharisee. In both cases priorities are all wrong.

The Pharisee

The Pharisee is the person who has a critical spirit and attempts to bully others into conforming to his thinking. Such a person must be resisted, especially at the point where he begins to exert an unhealthy influence over the weak. We must seek to instruct his conscience from the Bible, as far as we can, so that his moral record conforms more accurately to what is found there. In practice, the Pharisee will not always reveal himself straight away. We usually have to begin by assuming that we are dealing with a weaker brother or sister. Our priority, therefore, must be love, love for our fellow believer. The person must be educated from God's Word and that is to be done with love. As Paul says, we must speak the truth in love (Ephesians 4:15). We should avoid a scolding attitude. Such people must be lovingly brought to see that (Romans 14:17)

> ... the kingdom of God is not a matter of eating and drinking, but of righteousness, peace and joy in the Holy Spirit,

Hallesby advises anyone in this position not to

> consult more than one spiritual adviser and preferably one who is experienced and truly wise. But consult such a person often and be candid with him. Let him enlighten you from the Word of God and the experience of older Christians. If you have found a loving, wise and firm spiritual adviser you will with his help and intercession little by little be set free from the hindrances which are annoying you and come into the persuasion of a sound and healthy conscience.

Of course, there are dangers even in this approach but where it is taken as a short term expedient rather than a way of life over months or years and where the adviser truly is wise and wants to encourage an adult, mature biblical use of conscience then good will surely come out of such an arrangement.

The Eclectic society

The Eclectic Society was originally founded in London in 1783 by a number of ministers, chiefly Anglicans. Early members included hymn writer John Newton and Bible commentator Thomas Scott. The society met fortnightly to discuss pastoral and theological matters. On March 16, 1812, the subject for discussion was 'Wherein does a truly religious tenderness of conscience consist and how is it to be distinguished from (over)scrupulosity of conscience?' This is a great question, as we can see from what has been said so far in this chapter. Brief notes of the proceedings of the society were usually kept and later published. Some of the helpful remarks made on that occasion included 12 distinctions which we summarise below.

1. Rule. Tenderness of conscience regards God's rule. Scrupulosity frequently regards rules of its own traditions.

2. Meaning. Tenderness of conscience takes the obvious bearing of God's rule. St Paul would urge the spirit of a rule.

Scrupulosity generally rests itself on far-fetched inferences from the rule.

3. Light. Tenderness of conscience desires light.

Scrupulosity is frequently obstinate and unwilling to admit light.

4. Weight. Tenderness of conscience deals chiefly with the weightier matters of the law, the inside of the cup and platter.

Scrupulosity principally deals with trifles; the outside.

5. Spiritual. Tenderness of conscience has a tendency to promote the spiritual interests of the individual. Scrupulosity frequently has little or nothing to do with those interests.

6. Thoughts of others. Tenderness of conscience is candid and liberal toward others.

Scrupulosity is generally uncharitable in its judgement of others. It makes men offenders for a word.

7. Good of others. Tenderness of conscience is anxious to promote the spiritual good of others.

Scrupulosity is generally indifferent to such interests. It is zealous to win to a party.

8. Righteousness. Tenderness of conscience is associated with appropriate and full commitment to Christ.

Scrupulosity is self-righteous.

9. Universality. Tenderness of conscience has a universal regard to the commands of God.

Scrupulosity will sometimes take liberties beyond God's commands.

10. Tenderness of conscience respects the glory of God. Scrupulosity respects principally the honour that comes from man.

11. Tenderness of conscience is joined with humility and tenderness.

Scrupulosity, in the unconverted, with bigotry and pride.

12. Tenderness of conscience is attended with sympathy for the scruples of others.

Scrupulosity will anathematise other views.

The men also pointed out that tenderness and over-scrupulosity can sometimes live side by side in the same person and that Satan will try and lead the person with a tender conscience into over-scrupulosity, if he can.

It is important to maintain a distinction between a tender conscience and an over tender, a scrupulous or what we would call today an over-scrupulous one. In seeking to avoid having what we might best call an over-sensitive conscience we must not swing to the other extreme of having a conscience that is not sensitive enough. In the eighteenth century, giving advice to a young man, Isaac Watts once wrote

> Preserve your conscience always soft and sensible. If but one sin forces its way into that tender part of the soul, and dwell easy there, the road is paved for a thousand iniquities.

> And take heed that under any scruple, doubt or temptation whatsoever, you never let any reasonings satisfy your conscience, which will not be a sufficient answer or apology to the great Judge at the last day.

In this connection, the Victorian MP and philanthropist Charles Buxton is often quoted.

> *It is astonishing how soon the whole conscience begins to unravel if a single stitch drops.* One single sin indulged in makes a hole you could put your head through.

As we have said previously, the Christian must not go against his conscience. In Romans 14:23 Paul says regarding eating,

> But whoever has doubts is condemned if they eat, because their eating is not from faith; and everything that does not come from faith is sin.

To go against conscience will serve only to desensitise it. Certainly we want our consciences to be better and better informed but as one American quipped 'Quite often when a man thinks his mind is broadening it is more likely that his conscience is stretching'.

Commenting on Paul's understanding of conscience, Ridderbos has written that

> For a Christian *not a single decision* and action can be good which he does not think he can *justify on the ground* of his Christian conviction and his liberty before God in Christ.

The way forward on any given moral question is always to follow conscience proper, while carefully seeking to educate the moral record from what is in the Bible. Where changes are felt to be necessary these should be implemented with great care and much prayer. Sometimes there will need to be some sort of sensitive explanation to fellow believers of the changes in conviction that have led to the alterations in practice.

As the Apostle Paul says (Romans 14:5) 'Everyone should be sure about their beliefs in their own mind.'

9 Serve one another in love

Believers and differences of conscience

But this knowledge only fills people with pride. It is love that helps the church grow stronger. Those who think they know something do not yet know anything as they should.   1 Corinthians 8:1b–2

'… you don't always solve every problem with logic … A know-it-all attitude is only an evidence of ignorance.'   Warren Wiershe

It is clear from what has been said so far that although the conscience is a precious gift from God and a vital tool in the Christian's toolbox, it is far from perfect. The professing Christian can harden his conscience and even cauterise it so that it is practically useless. Even a well functioning conscience can be misinformed and advise something contrary to God's will. Although we must never go against our consciences, it is never enough simply to say 'my conscience says' or, as some make so bold to put it, 'God is telling me'. Rather, to the law and to the testimony. What does God's Word say?

Is a good conscience enough?

We have begun to look at Paul's teaching in 1 Corinthians 8–10. It is clear from those chapters that even a well-informed mind and conscience is not always enough to enable a person to make correct judgements about what he should or should not do in a given situation. This was the mistake that some of the Christians in Corinth made. They reasoned that as long as they knew what was right and were not going against their consciences, all must be well. They knew that an idol was nothing, so buying meat from the market place that may have been offered to an idol was no problem at all. In fact, some of them were so confident that even when they found themselves eating in an idol temple, as part of their civic duties perhaps, they still considered it not to be a problem at all.

And so today many Christians would be tempted to suppose that if they are not doing anything that is against their conscience and providing that they can see no biblical reason for supposing that their conscience is in error, then they must be free to go ahead and do as they wish. End of story. But is it?

If all Christians were equally strong in their convictions and equally well-informed from the Bible, then may be that would be the end of the story. However, that is not the case. There are, as we have seen, weaknesses of conscience—over-sensitivity, a certain instability. If strong believers carry on regardless of the existence of such weaker brothers and sisters then many professing Christians will not only be offended, but will be led to act against their consciences, so wounding or defiling them, or even, in a worst case scenario, somehow spiritually destroying themselves.

Sadly, this is all too often the case, especially in what Paul calls, in Romans 14, different ideas or disputable matters. It is all very well for the strong to say that the weak must grow up, that they need to be better informed and so on. However, where a matter is a disputable one, one on which there are differences, then it is clear that more information is never going to resolve such issues.

In Paul's day disputable matters included what food they could eat and what special days they should keep. Similarly, today there are disputes about what believers can eat, or more often, drink, or what days they should or should not mark and how they do that, as well as what exactly is or is not appropriate activity for the Lord's Day. Other obvious examples of disputable matters, perhaps, would be disagreements over appropriate clothing, jewellery or hairstyle, as well as what places a Christian may enter and to what types of music he can listen. Perhaps differences over Bible translations, subject and mode of baptism and even worship styles could to some extent come into the same category. It is possible to dispute what is disputable, of course!

The hope in all such disagreements should be that the strong will act towards the weak in the way that they are exhorted to act in the New Testament and that the weak will be kept from the twin evils of a tendency to Pharisaism, on the one hand, and of wounding or defiling their own consciences, on the other, if they are tempted to go against conscience.

Weakness and strength

Of course, when disputes occur, there can be an argument over who is weak and who is strong. Strength and weakness are not necessarily to be identified with respect to right and wrong. When a matter is disputable, such as that which exists today over the mode of baptism, each side will oppose the other and will usually argue that they have the Bible on their side. Weakness and strength then are to be understood rather in terms of stability of conviction and sensitivity of conscience. On the matter of baptism, if we can take that as an example, there are plenty of people with strong convictions on either side of the divide. No-one on either side should be tempted to change his view merely because some well known preacher takes the opposite view or because they read a few good arguments on the other side. There are some, however, who are not so strong and it is important that the strong do not take advantage of them.

An obvious example on this issue would be where a young person baptised as an infant and brought up in a home where they are considered to be in covenant with God finds themselves studying or working in a new town and, for want of a church more in line with their upbringing, starts attending a Baptist church. By the end of the first term, it may be, they are baptised by immersion, much to the chagrin of their parents and others back at home. However, hearing arguments from both sides, by Christmas (whether he or she celebrates it or not!) the young person is not sure what they believe about baptism any more.

Less obvious perhaps and less problematic in some ways but still undesirable is the scenario where the young person is brought up in a Baptist home, starts attending a Presbyterian church and espouses Presbyterian views, again much to the chagrin of his parents and others, but once again he is soon not sure what he believes about baptism.

We have already defined the chief characteristic of the weak Christian as not being wholly confident in his own opinion and therefore being likely to be swayed by others, namely the strong. Often, such a conscience is both ill-informed and over-sensitive. His misplaced priorities will often lead to legalism.

The strong Christian, by contrast, is a Christian whose conscience is well-informed from the Bible and who has begun to learn to enjoy his freedom in the Lord Jesus Christ without becoming over-sensitive about minor matters. Such people hope 'in God, not their money. Money cannot be trusted, but God takes care of us richly. He gives us everything to enjoy.' (1 Timothy 6:17). Ideally, he will have learned to be tolerant, recognising that mature Christians do differ on certain matters. He is not greatly offended when he comes across believers who differ with him on more secondary matters. Nor is he easily swayed when an argument that opposes his own views is powerfully presented, though he is open to change where that appears to be the right thing to do. He is not the sort of person who believes one thing one moment and something else the next.

Similarly, and this is Paul's concern in 1 Corinthians and in Romans, the strong Christian will not want to foist his ideas on others, ramrodding through his own view of a matter, regardless of the doubts and fears of the weaker Christian. The strong believer, if he really is strong in the best sense, will always have regard to the weak. It is never enough simply to know what is right and to be convinced in one's own conscience of its truth.

In 1953, Bible commentator F. W. Grosheide wrote

> The Corinthians had studied the question of the eating of sacrificed meat and they were convinced that they understood the problem except for a few minor details. But their starting point was all wrong. They began with the intellect ... Knowledge without love is sin (1 Corinthians 13:2, 8). The only right starting point is love.

To have proper Christian knowledge and wisdom, we need

also to have love, love for God and love for our fellow believers. If we simply stride ahead, doing all that our consciences will allow us to do without regard to the weak, we are going to sin against them and that is to sin against Christ (see 1 Corinthians 8:12). Such knowledge is liable to destroy the weak Christian by emboldening him to act against conscience. The exercise of my Christian freedom must never be allowed to be a stumbling block or a cause of sin to my weaker brother (1 Corinthians 8:9).

So, to take some obvious examples. Have you discovered from the Bible that it is okay for a Christian to drink wine or beer? Fine. But what if, in the exercise of that freedom, you encourage a less mature Christian to drink alcohol as well and it is against his conscience or he even gets drunk or perhaps begins to wander from the faith? If you are a Christian and you drink alcohol you need to be very careful that this does not become a stumbling block to others.

Are you a Christian who has no conscience about listening to any type of music? Fine. However, in exercising your freedom, are you in danger of encouraging some weaker Christian to espouse a certain lifestyle that is associated with the type of music that you prefer, one that will contribute eventually to that person's downfall?

This sometimes neglected aspect of Christian living is very important, especially in these days when so many have rediscovered the concept of Christian freedom and are glad to be throwing off the shackles of legalism. Too often activities that might have been alien to evangelical Christians 30 or 40 years ago are now not only treated as totally acceptable but seemingly accepted without the thought that they could be a stumbling block to younger, or sometimes, older Christians who are unaware of the dangers that lurk in every nook and cranny of the world around us.

So for example a young people's group from a local church may gather to watch a DVD or to see a film at the local cinema without any regard to the possibility that there may well be weaker Christians present who may be wounding their consciences by seeing such things or who may be led astray by the content of the film. The peer pressure experienced is likely to mean that they will not want to voice their uneasiness about what is happening and so there is an onus on the strong, especially the organisers of such an event, to think the matter through carefully. In many cases, much greater sensitivity is necessary.

Five responsibilities for the strong

If we turn again to Warren Wiersbe's little book on conscience , he usefully lists there five responsibilities for strong Christians in their dealings with the weak. Are we keeping these duties in mind?

- Accept him whose faith is weak (Romans 14:1, also 15:7). We do not have to immediately impress on everyone else what our consciences say. We should accept differences, especially on disputable matters. Here is a weak Christian who differs from me on baptism or church government. Do I say he cannot be a Christian? Not at all.

- Avoid arguments. Some people love to argue. It can be okay where two strong Christians disagree and want to thrash things out. But in an argument where the opponents are hopelessly mismatched, it is likely to lead to the wounding of the conscience of the weaker one. Romans 14:16 'do not let what you know is good be spoken of as evil.' Here is a brother who refuses to drink alcohol. You think he is far too fastidious. But he does it to God. It is to God that he will answer for his actions, not to you. Why would you want to encourage him to go against his conscience?

- Do not despise the weak. Romans 14:3–4, 10 says

> The one who eats everything must not treat with contempt the one who does not, and the one who does not eat everything must not judge the one who does, for God has accepted them. Who are you to judge someone else's servant? To their own master, servants stand or fall. And they will stand, for the Lord is able to make them stand … You, then, why do you judge your brother or sister? Or why do you treat them with contempt? For we will all stand before God's judgement seat.

How easy it is to have a condescending attitude towards other Christians, especially those who are young in the faith. 'How quaint his Sabbath scruples. If only he was as enlightened as me.'

'He will only use that version. If only he knew what I knew.' Avoid such attitudes.

- Do not make the weak stumble. Romans 14:13 and 15 says

> Therefore let us stop passing judgment on one another. Instead, make up your mind not to put any stumbling block or obstacle in the way of a brother or sister ... If your brother or sister is distressed because of what you eat, you are no longer acting in love. Do not by your eating destroy someone for whom Christ died.

Also see 14:23, which makes clear the danger

> But whoever has doubts is condemned if they eat, because their eating is not from faith; and everything that does not come from faith is sin.

Paul is not saying that we should not do anything of which we know another Christian would disapprove. Such a state of affairs would be impossible and would open the door to the tyranny of the Pharisee. No, the distress we are to avoid is the distress caused to a doubter when he violates his conscience by following the strong.

Here is a believer who refuses to watch TV or use the Internet. You take care how you use TV or the Internet but you have no problems with watching TV or using the Internet as such and so you talk endlessly in his presence about what you have seen on the box or on some website and how good it is. You may even be as insensitive as to invite him over to watch something on TV or put it on while he is in your home. A strong believer may take such an invitation as a harmless joke but to treat a weak brother in that way is to put a stumbling block before him that may lead to his eventual fall.

- Make peace. See Romans 14:19, 22

> Let us therefore make every effort to do what leads to peace and to mutual edification ... So whatever you believe about these things keep between yourself and God. Blessed is the one who does not condemn himself by what he approves.

To accept one another and to maintain Christian unity is a vital task. The responsibility for this lies chiefly with the strong.

You are concerned about a young person who does not use the Bible version you prefer or perhaps you object to his haircut or his clothes for some reason. Do you have to make an issue of it? They are not issues for him but they are for you and you want him to be conscientious about them. He fears, perhaps, that he will lose opportunities to witness to his friends if he goes against his conscience and makes the changes you recommend. And so there are arguments and bad feelings. Is that how the strong should act?

Paul's attitude, as outlined in 1 Corinthians 9, is a million miles from the condescending, dismissive and argumentative attitude shown by some modern Christians. Paul is pretty clear about what his rights are. In 1 Corinthians 9 he clearly shows that preachers should be financially provided for by those who hear them. However, and this is his point, Paul was not concerned about using those rights. He was willing to forgo them if it would be beneficial to the progress of the gospel. In 1 Corinthians 9:19 and 22 he says, strikingly, 'Though I am free and belong to no one, I have made myself a slave to everyone, to win as many as possible. ... I have become all things to all people so that by all possible means I might save some.'

These verses are often quoted in the context of evangelism, which is only the context here in part. The major context is Christian unity and the person to be won is probably already a Christian. Like Paul, we should aim to please everyone as far as we can (see 1 Corinthians 10:33). In our enthusiasm for Christian liberty we must not forget self-denial. Can we say what Paul says in 1 Corinthians 8:13?

> Therefore, if what I eat causes my brother or sister to fall into sin, I will never eat meat again, so that I will not cause them to fall.

Have we properly taken on board his statements in Romans 14:20–21 and 1 Corinthians 10:23–24?

> Do not destroy the work of God for the sake of food. All food is clean, but it is wrong for a person to eat anything that causes someone else to stumble. It is better not to eat meat or drink wine or to do anything else that will cause your brother or sister to fall.

'I have the right to do anything,' you say—but not everything is beneficial. 'I have the right to do anything'—but not everything is constructive. No one should seek their own good, but the good of others.

Some practical points from 1 Corinthians 10

How this works out in practice is taken up at the end of 1 Corinthians 10, from verse 23. There are four main things to notice.

- Do not wear your heart, which includes your conscience, on your sleeve. The Christian should not go looking for things to be conscientious about. As a general rule do not raise questions about food and drink and general lifestyle. As Psalm 24 begins 'The earth is the Lord's and everything in it'. That must be our starting point. The Kingdom of God is not chiefly about what you eat or drink or, for that matter, what you wear or what music you relax to (see Romans 14:17).

- Of course, the mature Christian is wise enough to know that certain situations are going to create difficulties and he is not to keep himself in ignorance. You are invited to a certain place, say, and you know that it is going to be dominated by unbelievers, perhaps a sports venue or some place of entertainment. It is surely wise to think through where you might be led into compromise, if you are not careful.

- When you are in such a situation, problems may arise. An unbeliever or another believer may raise a question of conscience—should we eat this food sacrificed to an idol, should we drink alcohol, should we dance or whatever? It is not that your conscience has any problem over the matter but now another person, believer or unbeliever, is raising issues, either because their conscience is troubled or because they think that this is a test case of whether you are living a Christian life or not. If you exercise your Christian freedom you may give the unbeliever an excuse to scorn Christianity if he is shocked by what you do or to be confused if he is sympathetic. Or you may put a stumbling block before the weak believer.

- This is not to allow our liberty to be judged by someone else. We are not saying that someone who takes a different view is right to denounce us for our attitude. The reason the strong believer forgoes his right is so that he does not cause his weaker brother or the unbeliever to stumble. When the weaker brother or the unbeliever is not around, the strong believer may eat or do whatever, as long as it is done thankfully and to the glory of God, with no questions raised.

One is conscious of the difficulty in presenting this material in a fair way that will be acceptable to all believers. Perhaps it is the very existence of the Pharisee and the weaker brother that makes such a task virtually impossible. It is unquestionably true, however, that we must seek to have a strong, though not a headstrong, conscience, that is one that is well informed and decided. A strong conscience is not everything, however, nor is Christian freedom. Love should be our highest goal.

Some practical points from Romans 14 and 15

To close let me re-iterate the five points that Garry Friesen makes from Romans 14 and 15.

- Learn to distinguish between matters of command and matters of freedom (14:14, 20)

In the church in Rome there were problems over what food to eat and what days to keep. These were disputable matters. The old commands about what food to eat and what days to keep were now gone with the bringing in of a new covenant and that left something of a vacuum. In the Corinthian church the matter of eating meat sacrificed to idols was the issue. There is no command that says 'Thou shalt not eat meat sacrificed to idols'. These matters then were matters of freedom not matters of command.

Sometimes distinguishing the two is not easy. Some see our attitude to the Lord's Day as a matter of command, something that carries over in part from the Old Testament. Others disagree and see it as a matter of freedom. Those who take it as a matter of command sometimes go on to see their way of keeping the day as a matter of command and fail to see that as a matter of freedom.

Whatever view we may take of baptism, we must recognise that as biblical as we may see our position to be and so a matter of command, salvation is not dependent on water. Whatever view we take, there must be some elements that are essential and some elements that are not of the essence of the thing.

- With regard to debatable issues, cultivate your own convictions. The whole of life must be lived to and for the Lord. He is the one who will be our Judge at the end. Christian freedom is to be enjoyed and those whose minds are filled with doubts are unstable and likely to fall. (14:5b)

- Allow your brother the freedom to determine his own convictions—even when they differ from yours. It is our duty to accept our brothers and sisters in Christ. They will also be judged by the Master whom they serve.

- Let your liberty be limited, when necessary, by love. 'For you' says Paul in Galatians 5:13 'were called to freedom, brothers. Only' he adds 'do not use your freedom as an opportunity for the flesh, but through love serve one another.' (14:1–12)

Follow Christ as the model and instructor of servanthood. (15:3–13). All his earthly life exemplifies the way the strong should act towards the weak.

10 Gimme a penny
Children and conscience

Train up a child in the way he should go; even when he is old he will not depart from it. Proverbs 22:6

'This God-given conscience is your ally in discipline and correction. Your most powerful appeals will be those that smite the conscience.' Tedd Tripp

An American writer tells the story of how at the Children's Hospital seven-year-old Jimmy was a constant troublemaker. One day a weekly visitor who knew him well said to him, 'Jimmy, if you are a good boy for a week, I will give you a quarter when I come back.' A week later she again stood by Jimmy's bed and said, 'Jimmy, I am not going to ask the nurse how you have behaved. You must tell me yourself. Do you deserve to have the quarter?' There was a moment's silence. Then from under the sheets came a small voice saying, 'Gimme a penny.' This illustrates how conscience speaks very clearly even in small children, and shows why God admonishes us to 'Train up a child in the way he should go; even when he is old he will not depart from it.' (Proverbs 22:6).

Alfred Rehwinkel rightly suggests that 'conscience develops in the individual like other faculties of the soul'. Just as a child is normally born a rational being, with all the powers and capacities of mind such as intellect, emotions and will, so from birth what we call conscience is also present. Further, just as the mental and emotional faculties of the child, present at birth, do not immediately function at full capacity but develop gradually as the child grows in body and mind, so conscience also needs to be developed.

Parents and others, such as teachers and ministers, influence the child's intellectual, emotional and volitional development. They must also take note of the influence that they are having on the development of the child's conscience. Usually it is the parents who provide the moral record for the child to react to in his conscience. They must be aware of this and at the same time that his ability to reason and judge develop so he will become conscious of his own behaviour and of his relation and obligations to others. He will begin to distinguish between right and wrong for himself and conscience will begin to assert itself.

Example

In a chapter on 'conscience at home' Robert Solomon begins by saying that because it is important for parents to train their children's conscience, they must first ensure that their own consciences are intact and functioning well.

Rehwinkel and others also remind us of the importance of the good example of parents, pastors, teachers and others. This matter of example applies to any Christian who comes into contact with a child, although in most cases it will be the parents' influence that is most significant. It must be borne in mind, says Rehwinkel, that 'children learn more by imitation than by rule and more by example than by precept'. Good examples will encourage the child to fear God and to honour him, bad ones, especially where hypocrisy and inconsistency are observed, will cause young people to be confused and uncertain about right and wrong and their consciences will then not develop as they should.

The little ones of Matthew 18:6–7 are probably believers but the warning is still worth pondering in relation to children

> But whoever causes one of these little ones who believe in me to sin, it would be better for him to have a great millstone fastened around his neck and to be drowned in the depth of the sea. Woe to

the world for temptations to sin! For it is necessary that temptations come, but woe to the one by whom the temptation comes!

Education

For children and adults alike, the conscience, as with other faculties of the soul, develops through exercising it. Children and young Christians must be brought up to exercise their conscience. This is done chiefly through Christian education and Christian discipline.

Parents must impress God's commands on their children, informing their moral record and giving them plenty of time to discuss these things, as is envisioned in Deuteronomy 6. By this means they will know how to employ conscience proper and have opportunity to be reminded of how to live in a right minded way, according to conscience.

The need to impress the truth on a child's mind was taken up by John King writing in the nineteenth century. He asks

> How many parents are solicitous to furnish the minds of their children with learning and accomplishments, who are all but absolutely indifferent to their moral training? The youthful intellect is cultivated perhaps to a sickly and exhausting luxuriance, while the conscience is left, in all the dreariness of a barren desert. The inferior powers are trained for mastery, the superior for servitude; as if it were the great object of parental solicitude, to counteract the law and ordinance of heaven, to thwart the design of infinite wisdom, and to

render their offspring as unlike what God intended them to be, as possible!

Rehwinkel draws attention to a magazine article from 1955. Frank Chodorov reported as follows

A New York judge, reflecting on the increase of juvenile delinquency, came up with the observation that not one Chinese-American boy had been brought before him in his seventeen years on the bench. Remarking on this fact to other judges, he learned that their experience coincided with his. Chicago and San Francisco authorities reported likewise.

P. H. Chang, Chinese consul-general in New York City, was asked to comment on this. He apparently said, according to the Saturday Evening Post of the time,

A Chinese child, no matter where he lives, is brought up to recognize that he cannot shame his parents ... Before a Chinese child makes a move, he stops to think what the reaction of his parents will be. Will they be proud or will they be ashamed? That is the sole question he asks himself.

The argument is anecdotal but it suggests that a diligent and careful discipline in the early years can have quite a marked effect. Children crave moral guidance and love to know the rules. How difficult for the child who is not taught right from wrong. The happiest children are those, no doubt, who know exactly where the boundaries are, whether they choose to test them or not. 'When moral discipline is neglected,' says Rehwinkel 'the child's conscience cannot develop. It will remain weak, uncertain and confused, and will be unable to serve as a strong monitor in a moral crisis.'

Entreaty

One of the best books on raising children to appear in recent years is Tedd Tripp's *Shepherding a child's heart*. In it he points out that for correction and discipline to be effective, it must be directed to the child's conscience. 'Your correction and discipline must find their mark in the conscience of your son or daughter'. The conscience is the parent's ally in discipline and correction. Nothing is more powerful than an appeal to the child's conscience.

Tripp points out that if you go to Proverbs 23, the stand out verses for a parent are probably verses 13 and 14

> Do not withhold discipline from a child; if you strike him with a rod, he will not die. If you strike him with the rod, you will save his soul from Sheol.

However, many other verses in the chapter are relevant and model the appeal to the conscience. 'Let not your heart envy sinners ... direct your heart in the way ... Listen to your father, who gave you life ... Buy truth and do not sell it; buy wisdom, instruction and understanding ... My son, give me your heart ...' (see verses 17, 19, 22, 23 and 26). 'The passage actually drips with sweet and tender entreaty that appeals to the conscience' says Tripp, 'the rod gets the attention, but the conscience must be ploughed up and planted with the truth of God's way.'

He also argues from the Gospels, and Matthew 21 in particular, pointing out examples of where Jesus, in his parables of the two sons and of the tenants, makes his appeal to conscience, thus dealing 'with the root problems, not just the surface issues'. Tripp rightly says that parents need to work in the same way.

He wisely says too that 'if you make your appeal there, you avoid making correction a contest between you and your child. Your child's controversy is always with God.' He also points out that in correction parents need to get beyond the outward issues of behaviour and address the issues of the heart. It is by appealing to the child's conscience that they will be able to do this.

To re-enforce his point he tells the story of an incident where a young boy was found stealing money from the offering plate after the church service. The father was informed and shortly after he and his son appeared in the pastor's study where the boy produced $2 and confessed to having taken it. He was in tears and asking for forgiveness. The pastor told him he was glad that in God's mercy the boy had been caught. God had spared him the hardness of heart that comes when a person sins and gets away with it.

He then went on to remind him why Jesus came. It is because people like him and his father and the pastor have hearts that want to steal but God's love for wicked boys and men is so great that he sent his Son to change them from the inside out and make them givers not takers.

It was only at this point that the boy broke down in sobs and took a further $20 from his pocket! Up until then he had merely been going through the motions. 'What happened?' asks Tripp. Clearly the boy's conscience 'was smitten by the gospel! ... The gospel hit its mark in his conscience'. Conscience had done something that a beating would never have done.

Tripp concludes

> You must address the heart as the fountain of behaviour, and the conscience as the God-given judge of right and wrong. You can't be with him all the time. He must know what to do in situations that you cannot anticipate. He needs biblical wisdom. His conscience must develop as the reasoning factor of the soul so that he will know what he ought to do even when you are not there.

Gary Ezzo, another popular writer in this area, has also written on the importance of conscience in bringing up children. He has been accused by some of Freudianism in some of his writing but his distinction between negative and positive conscience training is useful.

Negative training consists of warnings, restrictions and consequences while positive training consists of instruction, showing the moral reasoning behind a parents' instructions, encouragement and reinforcement. He suggests that negative training should predominate in the early years and positive training in the middle and upper childhood years. He identifies the age of three as the time when the transition should begin. The idea is to move from the prohibitive fear 'I must or else ...' to the positive 'I must because it's right ...' Parents need to work toward the positive.

Habit

One way of describing what parents and other carers need to be doing is to say that they should be aiming to inculcate good habits in children and young people. A habit is something that has become automatic through repetition. God has made us in such a way that we are creatures of habit—habits good or bad. We can develop physical, mental, moral and spiritual habits, and these can be good or bad. It is part of the parent's remit to develop good habits in those they care for.

Rehwinkel says that an 'abundance of good habits is a great asset to an individual'. The nineteenth century writer Charles Reade is often credited with the saying 'sow a habit, and you reap a character; sow a character, and you reap a destiny'. In other words, character is the sum total of our habits.

The world is pretty convinced with regard to the power of habit in regard to learning to spell, doing arithmetic and learning to play a musical instrument. When it comes to mental attitudes and spiritual habits, right emotion and spiritual strengths, we seem to be less clear on the importance of habit formation.

Rehwinkel says that 'parents are directly responsible for the habits formed by their children, including the moral and religious habits'. If this is true, then parents who provide their children with a stock of good habits have provided them with armour that will stand the test when tried. Joseph is an obvious example of how this works in Scripture. Samuel and Timothy are other examples. If parents fail to do this, they fail in their greatest responsibility, and their children are left inadequate to face the moral hazards that exist in this world.

Heart change

Later in his book Tripp comes back to the subject of conscience when he talks about the need for heart change in every child. As we have said earlier in this book, heart change begins with conviction of sin and that happens in the conscience. To help children towards this, parents must appeal to the conscience. Like Rehwinkel, Tripp is eager that parents deal with issues of character not mere outward behaviour. In order to do that, they must learn how to appeal to the conscience. 'If you wish to deal with character and not just with behaviour, you must deal with the child in a deep way that enables him to see the implications of his behaviour and to indict himself.'

By way of example he takes the parable of the Good Samaritan and the appeal to conscience found there, the parable of the unmerciful servant and the way Jesus deals with Simon the Pharisee in Luke 7.

He reminds parents

> Your child's controversy is always with God. Dealing with children in this way avoids giving them a keepable standard so that they feel smug and righteous. They are faced with God's ways and how much they need the radical, renovating work of Christ. When your child has come (by the work of the Holy Spirit and the exercise of the means God has ordained for nurturing children) to see his sinfulness, you must point him to Jesus Christ, the only Saviour of humankind. Strive to help your child, who is a selfish sinner, see his need of Christ's grace and mercy in the cross.

Tripp often raises the classic question of how you deal with children in a dispute over a toy. He rightly points out that the question of who had it first does not deal with the issue. Rather, we must address the selfish heart from which such disputes flow. If we do not, we will never lead a child to the cross.

Dealing with the real issues of the heart opens the way continually to the cross where forgiveness is found for twisted, warped and sinful boys and girls. Truly Christian responses cannot be produced legalistically because they deal with attitudes, not just with the external behaviour.

We mentioned Mark Twain's novel *Huckleberry Finn* in a

previous chapter. The book shows a remarkable ability to get into the mind of a young boy. In one place Twain has Huck say to the reader (using language to refer to a black man acceptable then but not today).

That's just the way: a person does a low-down thing, and then he don't want to take no consequences of it. Thinks as long as he can hide, it ain't no disgrace. That was my fix exactly. The more I studied about this the more my conscience went to grinding me, and the more wicked and low-down and ornery I got to feeling. And at last, when it hit me all of a sudden that here was the plain hand of Providence slapping me in the face and letting me know my wickedness was being watched all the time from up there in heaven, whilst I was stealing a poor old woman's nigger that hadn't ever done me no harm, and now was showing me there's One that's always on the lookout, and ain't agoing to allow no such miserable doings to go only just so fur and no further, I most dropped in my tracks I was so scared. Well, I tried the best I could to kinder soften it up somehow for myself by saying I was brung up wicked, and so I warn't so much to blame; but something inside of me kept saying, 'There was the Sunday-school, you could a gone to it; and if you'd a done it they'd a learnt you there that people that acts as I'd been acting about that nigger goes to everlasting fire.'

It is a reminder of the powerful workings of conscience that the young can experience, even those that do not attend Sunday School. However, before we think that heart change comes easily, the chapter concludes, following the reference to everlasting fire, like this.

It made me shiver. And I about made up my mind to pray, and see if I couldn't try to quit being the kind of a boy I was and be better. So I kneeled down. But the words wouldn't come. Why wouldn't they? It warn't no use to try and hide it from Him. Nor from *me*, neither. I knowed very well why they wouldn't come. It was because my heart warn't right; it was because I warn't square; it was because I was playing double. I was letting *on* to give up sin, but away inside of me I was holding on to the biggest one of all. I was trying to make my mouth *say* I would do the right thing and the clean thing, and go and write to that nigger's owner and tell where he was; but deep down in me I knowed it was a lie, and He knowed it. You can't pray a lie—I found that out.

Writing for children in 1838, Peter Parley concludes the Bible story of Herod's murder of John the Baptist by asking 'Does my little reader know what conscience is?' He explains very simply

> When you are naughty, there is something in your heart which makes you feel you are doing wrong and offending against Heaven.

> And when you correct yourself, and try to be good, you feel happy and cheerful. Well, that something—that feeling—in your heart, which makes you happy when you are good, and unhappy when you

are naughty, is your conscience; and it is God Himself who has put it there …

He concludes by saying that conscience is a voice 'which you ought always to obey'. This is a good example of how we might introduce the idea to a child.

Isaac Watts' earlier poem for children is now rather dated but its sentiments are still appropriate and might make a fitting conclusion to this chapter.

> When a foolish thought within
> It tries to take us in a snare,
> Conscience tells us, 'It is sin,'
> And entreats us to beware.
> If in something we transgress,
> And are tempted to deny;
> Conscience says, 'Your faults confess,
> Do not dare to tell a lie.'
>
> In the morning, when we rise,
> And would fain omit to pray,
> 'Child, consider,' Conscience cries,
> 'Should not God be sought to-day?'
> When within His holy walls,
> Far abroad our thoughts we send,
> Conscience often loudly calls,
> And entreats us to attend.

When our angry passions rise,
Tempting to revenge an ill,
'Now subdue it,' Conscience cries,
'Do command your temper still.'
But if we should disregard,
While those friendly voices call.
Conscience soon will grow so hard
That it will not speak at all.

11

Jesus is Lord
The state and liberty of conscience

We must obey God rather than men! Acts 5:29

'God needeth not the help of a material sword of steel to assist the sword of the Spirit in the affairs of conscience.'

Roger Williams

Conscience is often discussed in relation to the matter of civil and religious liberty and the vexed issue of the relationship between the church and the state. It is good to include a chapter on this sometimes difficult but always important subject.

Hot topic

Back at the end of the sixties Sir Fred Catherwood reminded us that this matter of state toleration is

> an issue upon which Christians must always be alert. It does not come naturally to man. It comes with difficulty even to Christians. Protestants had to wait for a century after the Reformation before the principle became established and even then they had to fight continually to see that it was maintained.

The topic is a hot one today for Christians around the world. In the democratic west, believers find themselves increasingly forced to follow their consciences against state laws or more often against the way those laws are applied. In other parts of the world, such as North Korea and parts of China, the state still actively persecutes people who would dare to conscientiously disagree with its policies. Then there are countries where a religious fundamentalism of one sort or another has taken hold and the power of the state is used to suppress the gospel or is at least unavailable to protect the Christian minority. There are still countries too where the so-called church is eager to ally itself with the state in opposition to the religious liberty of true believers.

Meanwhile, post-modernism and the mindset that denies all absolute moral truth is also rampant in many places. It is claimed that individuals are shaped wholly by cultural forces. Will those whose concept of civil and religious liberties is that it is a mere construct born of a particular culture and not universally valid for all cultures care about what happens to others or champion the rights of the individual conscience before the state or other authorities? Will they advocate civil and religious liberty and freedom of conscience for all?

Terms

A number of terms are in use in connection with liberty of conscience in relation to the state. In a series of lectures given to young men in New York in the 1830s Gardiner Spring spoke both of civil and religious liberty. Civil liberty, he felt, is enjoyed in its highest degree 'where natural liberty is so far only abridged and restrained, as is necessary and expedient for the safety and interest of the society or State.' People speak more often today perhaps of civil liberties, civil rights or human rights.

As for religious liberty or freedom, Gardiner Spring calls it

> the right of every man to adopt and enjoy whatever opinions he chooses on religious subjects, and to worship the Supreme Being according to the dictates of his own conscience, without any obstruction from the law of the land.

He distinguishes the two, saying that 'Civil liberty relates to things seen and temporal, religious liberty to things unseen and eternal'.

Like others he is also keen to distinguish between liberty and toleration. Christians differ on this but for Spring, religious toleration only allows religious opinions and forms of worship different to those established by law, whereas religious liberty 'disclaims all right of law to control men in their opinions and worship'. While toleration 'implies the existence and the modified exercise of power in such control', liberty 'implies that no such power exists, and none such is assumed'. He sees the ideal as being when one religious denomination has as good a right as another, to the free and unobstructed enjoyment of its creed and worship.

The distinction between toleration and liberty explains why the Baptist John Leland could say, in 1790, 'the very idea of toleration is despicable; it supposes that some have a pre-eminence above the rest to grant indulgence, whereas all should be equally free, Jews, Turks, Pagans and Christians.' The problem with the statement is that it gives the impression that the views of Jews, Muslim, Pagans and Christians are all ultimately valid, which no Christian can accept. This is why many prefer the word toleration.

Church and state

Don Carson reminds us that

> Every Culture and every age necessarily displays some tolerance and some intolerance. No culture can be tolerant of everything or intolerant of everything: it is simply not possible.

Down the years, however, various views on how church and state should relate have made for clear differences in the way nations have approached toleration. Using very broad brush strokes, we can identify at least four major approaches.

1. The state is subservient to the church. This is the view that prevailed in Mediaeval times in Europe when the Roman Catholic church held sway. Jesuit Cardinal Robert Bellarmine (1542–1621) went as far as to say that the Pope has, 'in order to spiritual good, the supreme power to dispose of the temporal affairs of all Christians'.

2. The church is part of the state and so subservient to it. This is called Erastianism (named for Zwinglian theologian Thomas Erastus 1524–1583). Leaders in the church get all their power from the state. The magisterial Reformers never really got away from this outlook and understanding.

3. The church and state are separate but must work hand in hand as an alliance. This perhaps best expresses the post-Reformation view of the Presbyterians. Church and State have different origins, different objects, different powers and different means of administration but should work together as friends.

4. The church and state are separate and operate in different spheres. This is the view, after the Reformation, of Independents and Baptists and the view taken up in America and that, in secularised from, prevails in most democracies today.

For those who want to be bound by the Bible it is only these latter two views that offer anything like a view that is compatible with what we read of in the New Testament.

The Bible never says, as the Baptist Barrett Duke notes, that God wants all people to be free to worship or not to worship whatever they want. Or as another Baptist, the late J. D. Hughey, put it 'religious liberty is not a truth explicitly revealed in Scripture'. However, both men agree that 'religious liberty is implicit in Christian teaching' and both argue for it on the basis of Christian doctrines such as the doctrine of God, of man, of Christ, of salvation and so on.

There are plenty of verses in the Bible that suggest God has granted mankind the freedom to choose who or what he wants to worship, as he pleases. When we add what it says about conscience there are good arguments for civil and religious liberty. In 1 Corinthians and Romans Paul teaches that none of us is to create a situation where we needlessly offend or interfere with the conscience of an individual in the church. Surely we can rightly extend the argument to provide what is a fundamental ground for religious and civil liberties.

Biblical material

As for more specific biblical material on this matter, we will find little to help us in the period when the nation of Israel was being founded and established as it is clear that at that time church and state were one in a way that was not intended to last. Even in that dispensation, however, kingship and priesthood were very clearly demarcated.

One of the big differences between Roger Williams (c 1604–1683) and John Cotton (1585–1652) who we will look at later in this chapter was on this question of how to handle the Old Testament. For Williams 'The Pattern of the National Church of Israel, was ... unimitable by any Civil State'. To use the Old Testament to justify the punishment by the state of heretics and blasphemers or to force people to go to church by law, as was done in Massachusetts at the time, was illegitimate, for Williams.

When we come to the Book of Daniel, however, and the exile to Babylon we have more than one incident where the faithful are confronted by a hostile state, and faced with a conflicting law have to choose to go with what conscience says rather than what the law says.

In Chapter 1 Daniel and his friends draw a line in the sand regarding what they will eat and drink. They make it a matter of conscience and, despite the scepticism of their Babylonian instructor, are vindicated.

Then famously, in Daniel 3, the three friends are commanded to bow down to Nebuchadnezzar's statue and worship it. With quiet dignity they refuse the order, to the King's exasperation, even though they are threatened with apparently certain death in the fiery furnace. Their words to the pagan king are wise and powerful. They say

> O Nebuchadnezzar, we have no need to answer you in this matter. If this be so, our God whom we serve is able to deliver us from the burning fiery furnace, and he will deliver us out of your hand, O king. But if not, be it known to you, O king, that we will not serve your gods or worship the golden image that you have set up. (Daniel 3:16–18)

Of course, the friends are wonderfully vindicated but it is clear that this was not their motivation but a refusal to compromise conscience regardless of the consequences.

Even more famously, something similar happens to Daniel himself in his old age in Chapter 6. This time the King is Darius the Mede and although he is the victim of a political intrigue he ends up in the same position as Nebuchadnezzar before him—demanding worship that the faithful are rightly unwilling to give. The threat of death in a lions' den holds no more terror for Daniel than the fiery furnace did for his friends. 'Refusing to let the state dictate the nature, content, or timing of his prayer life,' as it has been put, Daniel boldly continued to open his windows towards Jerusalem and pray on his knees three times a day to his God, just as he had done previously.

The attitude seen in Daniel and his friends is seen also in the New Testament apostles. First, in Acts 4 they are banned from preaching in the name of Jesus following the healing of the man at the Temple gate. In verses 19 and 20 Peter and John refuse to comply with the demands of the Sanhedrin with great eloquence and power. They say

> Whether it is right in the sight of God to listen to you rather than to God, you must judge, for we cannot but speak of what we have seen and heard.

In Acts 5 they are again brought before the civil authorities, who, motivated by jealousy, again command them to stop preaching about Jesus. Rather than accept this, they respond with another wonderful statement, saying 'we must obey God rather than men' (Acts 5:29).

These Scriptures along with Jesus' statement that we must give to Caesar what is Caesar's and to God what is his and the way that Paul actively sought the protection of the pagan Roman state in the church's early years should convince all Christians that the state can protect Christians as long as it does not put itself above God.

John 18:36 also has something to say to this. Jesus says 'My kingdom is not of this world. If my kingdom were of this world, my servants would have been fighting, that I might not be delivered over to the Jews. But my kingdom is not from the world.' The church is never at liberty to seek to advance the kingdom by means of the sword or any other act of coercion. In 2 Corinthians 10:4

Paul says that 'the weapons of our warfare are not of the flesh'. Jesus rebuked James and John when they wanted to call down fire on the Samaritans (Luke 9:54). What a terrible mistake when the professed church has forgotten this, as in the crusades.

Luke 12:13–14 is interesting here too. Jesus refuses to cast judgement in a dispute between two brothers that is brought to his attention. He asks, 'who made me a judge or arbitrator over you?'

Passages in Romans 13 and 1 Peter clearly encourage all due respect for the powers that be and show that the state has the right to use the sword to legitimately enforce its own authority—but not that of the church. 1 Timothy 2 also urges us to pray for such leaders with the progress of the gospel in mind. Romans 13:5 argues significantly that 'one must be in subjection, not only to avoid God's wrath but also for the sake of conscience'.

It is also surely clear that the nature of faith itself, as revealed in the Bible, is repugnant to the very idea of using any form of coercion to bring it about or to sustain it. Each individual will one day have to stand before God and give a personal accounting.

Clearly church and state operate in different spheres and their authority should be kept separate. This separation does not preclude Christians as individuals, especially in a democracy, doing all they can to argue for government that is in line with the basic norms found in Scripture.

Down the years and even to the present day many believers have taken the sort of stand Daniel and his friends and the Apostles took when commanded by the state to do what is clearly against their biblically informed consciences. To take just one example. In Foxe's *Acts and Monuments* he describes how a gathered church that was meeting in Islington, then a village outside London, was surprised and 40 were arrested. Some 27 were summoned to appear before Sir Roger Cholmly, and 22 ended up spending seven weeks in Newgate prison until they were examined. The prison keeper informed them that all that was required of them was to hear Mass.

'Easy as this condition may seem' comments Foxe 'these martyrs valued their purity of conscience more than loss of life or property' and so, although seven were providentially preserved, two died in prison, and 13 were burnt at Smithfield and Brentford.

Learning from history

The first time conscience in matters of faith was officially placed centre stage, Dr Duke suggests, was in 1612 when a confession appeared called 'Propositions and Conclusions concerning True Christian Religion, containing a Confession of Faith of certain English people, living at Amsterdam.' Lumpkin's collection of Baptist creeds suggests it may have been a modification of a confession written in Dutch by John Smyth, a principal leader in the group that would become the General Baptists. Estep says it definitely was his work. The confession says

That the magistrate is not by virtue of his office to meddle with religion, or matters of conscience, to force or compel men to this or that form of religion, or doctrine: but to leave Christian religion free, to every man's conscience, and to handle only civil transgressions (Romans 13:1), injuries and wrongs of man against man, in murder, adultery, theft, etc., for Christ only is king and lawgiver of the church and conscience (James 4:12).

Lumpkin calls it 'perhaps the first confession of faith of modern times to demand freedom of conscience and separation of church and state.'

He has to say 'modern times' because good statements can be found as far back as Tertullian, who wrote that 'it is a fundamental human right, a privilege of nature, that every man should worship according to his own convictions' and protested against being forced by the Romans to worship what he had no wish to worship.

Among works cited by Carson in his brief history of the subject in *The Intolerance of Tolerance* are the *Areopagitica* by John Milton (1608–1674), a 1644 work that vigorously defended freedom of speech and expression and that was immediately popular. He says that Samuel Rutherford''s *A Free Disputation against Pretended Liberty of Conscience* five years later is essentially a reply, advocating that the Christian State demand outward conformity even though inward conformity is what ultimately matters. Milton later named Rutherford in a hostile sonnet against *The New Forcers of Conscience under the Long Parliament*. A later writer on

Rutherford's side was Richard Baxter (1615–1691) who wrote in *A Holy Commonwealth* that 'liberty in all matters of worship and of faith, is the open and apparent way to set up Popery in the land …'

Carson also mentions John Locke and John Owen and Roger Williams in New England who argued for religious liberty in his famous work also from 1644 *The Bloudy Tenent of Persecution*. His opponent was John Cotton who wrote *The Bloudy Tenent, Washed and made white in the bloode of the Lambe,* Williams responding with *The Bloudy Tenent Yet More Bloudy* in 1652.

Roger Williams

Writing on Williams' moral theology in 2004, James Calvin Davis suggests that Williams' views provide a third way between what he calls today's Christian particularists 'who argue that the meaning of Christian ethics is bound and limited to its context in the communion of faith' and, what he calls strict universalists, who assert the need to transcend such limits.

Williams' main arguments for liberty of conscience and separation of church and state are distilled in Davis' book and have been summarised in a paper by Mostyn Roberts under three headings and with two brief additions.

Conscience

Cotton was happy to say that no man should be persecuted for conscience's sake but goes on to say that if such a person continues to deny fundamental principles of doctrine and worship that the

Bible is clear on then he is no longer acting out of conscience but against it! His proof text is Titus 3:10 on how to deal with divisive persons. The context, of course, is church discipline so Cotton is clearly conflating church and state. The implications are that only someone who takes Cotton's view can have a good conscience, to be unorthodox is to sin against conscience and the conscience is quite different to what we have seen it to be in this book.

What Williams wants is a situation where mind and will act together. His idea of conscience has more to do with the mind, Cotton's is more to do with the will. Surely, as stated previously, to encourage a person to go against his conscience can never be right.

Williams defined conscience as 'a *persuasion* fixed in the mind and heart of a man which enforceth him to judge ... and to do so and so, with respect to God, his worship, etc ... As Matthew Henry would later, he spoke of it as 'the candle of the Lord' in the human heart. Like other Puritans he accepted its universal presence in men, as is seen in the way he dealt with the Native Americans. Roberts says that 'he believed that the Indians not only valued mature moral conscience more than the English but they also showed more respect for variations in conscience than he observed in his own society.'

His arguments for the inviolability of conscience include the fact God alone is its Lord; the ineffectiveness of attempts at coercion; the danger of promoting hypocrisy and hardening people in their erroneous convictions or encouraging them to trample over conscience. He could see how such a policy might eventually turn against the true church and how it tended to bankrupt society.

Williams did not suppose that freedom of conscience was unlimited. Even he could see that there were situations where there was no alternative to coercion. Nevertheless he was way ahead of his time in his understanding of how men and women of very diverse beliefs can reasonably co-exist.

Church and State

It is not true to say that the Puritans failed to distinguish between church and state. From Calvin on, the best of the Reformed were clear on this. It is only a matter of degree. Because Williams' great concern was always worship and faith, the workings and relationship of the soul towards God, he thought differently. He felt this was an area where the state has no right to interfere and this is why early on he proclaimed that the state had no right to enforce the first table of the law.

He was no anarchist. He was quite happy for the state to outlaw, say, human sacrifice or prostitution. He made a big point from the parable of the wheat and the tares or weeds that the field is the world not the church. It is wrong to punish heretics and blasphemers in the world, whatever one does as far as church discipline is concerned. Their day of judgement will come soon enough.

The State a Nursing Father to the Church

Williams challenged the widespread Puritan view that the state was responsible to God for the religion and morality of the nation and that it had a right to try and ensure by force that true religion and godliness were maintained. He had many arguments against this view.

First—government is a creation ordinance and is known among pagans as well as among Christians. Further, unbelievers often make good governors, why pass them by? History teaches us that when the state is asked to look after the church, it inevitably happens that by degrees 'the gardens of churches of the saints' are 'turned into the wilderness of whole nations until the whole world' becomes 'Christian, or Christendom'. Like many others since, Williams saw what happened in the Roman Empire under Constantine as a disaster for the church. The history of England since Henry VIII is surely very instructive on that score.

He did not deny that the government should encourage and protect true religion by protecting freedom of religion, but he saw no need for their superintendence over it.

Two images convey this all very well. Firstly, a city. In a famous passage Williams says

> The Church or company of worshippers, whether true or false, is like unto a body or college of physicians in a city—like unto a corporation, society or company of East India or Turkey merchants,

or any other society or company in London: which companies may hold their courts, keep their records, hold disputations, and in matters concerning their society may dissent, divide, break into schisms and factions, sue and implead each other at the law, yea, wholly dissolve and break up into pieces and nothing, and yet the peace of the city not be in the least measure impaired or disturbed; because the essence or being of the city and so the well being and peace thereof is essentially distinct from those particular societies ...

Writing to the town of Providence in 1655, he asserted his firm belief in civil government in its rightful place, using the image of a ship

There goes many a ship to sea, with many hundreds of souls in one ship, whose weal and woe is common, and a true picture of a commonwealth, or a human combination or society. It hath fallen out sometimes that both Papists and Protestants, Jews and Turks, may be embarked in one ship, upon which supposal I affirm, that all the liberty of conscience I ever pleaded for, turns upon these two hinges: that none of the Papists, Protestants, Jews or Turks be forced to come to the ship's prayers or worship, nor compelled from their own particular prayers or worship, if they practise any. I further add, that I never denied, that notwithstanding this liberty, the commander of this ship ought to command the ship's course, yes, and also command that justice, peace and sobriety be kept and practised, both among the seamen and all the passengers. If any of the seamen refuse to perform their service, or passengers to pay their freight; if any refuse to help in person or purse towards the common charges or defence; if any refuse to obey the common laws and orders of the ship, concerning the common peace or preservation; if any shall rise up against their commanders and officers, if any should preach or write that there ought to be no commanders or officer, because all are equal in Christ, therefore no masters of or officers, no laws, no orders, no corrections, nor punishments; I say I never denied but in such cases, whatever is pretended, the commander and or commanders may judge, resist, compel and punish such transgressors, according to their deserts and merits.

Pluralism and natural law

Davis also points to two other things in Williams. One of the problems with pluralism is to know on what moral basis a society is to be built. Williams was quite happy to say it is natural law. He believed that to some extent God's absolute moral law is embedded in every human being and is reflected in conscience. He took into account not only what the Bible says but the witness of history and of his own experience with the Indians. This convinced him that civil government can exist where there is no gospel. By distinguishing between the church and the world Williams could allow freedom of conscience without fear that God will be dishonoured or true religion suffer.

Civility

Williams was fond of the word civility to describe the pattern of life in a society governed by the second table of the law, or to be exact these rules—murder, adultery, theft and lying are wrong and justice is a 'Golden Rule' or principle in society—do as you would be done by. He was also in favour of virtues such as sociableness, neighbourliness, loyalty, dependability, respect for civil authority and gratitude.

One may not agree with all that Williams wrote and applying it to the situation today is not always easy but he certainly gives us a good outline of what we ought to be aiming at. The subject is difficult but surely the separation of church and state is a New Testament doctrine, as is the idea that the state cannot coerce its citizens and bind their consciences where they are not in opposition to God's law. Conscience should be free.

12 And the books were opened
Eternity and conscience

... where their worm does not die and the fire is not quenched.
Mark 9:48

His master said to him, 'Well done, good and faithful servant. You have been faithful over a little; I will set you over much. Enter into the joy of your master.'
Matthew 25:21

'Without conscience there could be no hell of remorse, and without conscience there could be no heaven of bliss.'
Charles H. Pridgeon

A proper study of the Bible's teaching on conscience would be incomplete without some consideration of conscience in eternity. We have considered conscience before the fall and after it, conscience in the believer and in the unbeliever on earth, finally we come to conscience in the believer and in the unbeliever after death.

Conscience in eternity

Although it is often attacked, the doctrine of the immortality of the soul is biblical. When Augustine said in his *City of God* that the soul

> is therefore called immortal, because in a sense, it does not cease to live and to feel; while the body is called mortal because it can be forsaken of all life, and cannot by itself live at all

he wrote what is in line with what the Bible actually teaches.

We must certainly see the emphasis in Scripture on bodily resurrection and not import into our thinking ideas that are Greek rather than Christian. However, both in the Old Testament and the New there are verses that point to the soul's immortality. Ecclesiastes 12:7 talks about death taking place when the dust returns 'to the earth as it was' and the spirit returns 'to God who gave it'. In Luke 12:4 we read Jesus' statement that we should 'not fear those who kill the body and after that have nothing more they can do', implying that the soul lives on beyond physical death.

Paul's statement in 2 Corinthians 5:8 about being absent from the body but present with the Lord points us in the same direction.

If the soul lives on after death then, logically, the conscience lives on too. The Bible requires us to believe in the immortality of the conscience. John King said of it that it is 'like the other noble powers of his mind, indestructible.' He wrote that

> Neither life nor death, nor time nor eternity, nor the happiness of heaven, nor the misery of hell, will be able to extinguish this spark of moral life within the human breast. Conscience has, and will have a voice, which the extremes of exultation and of horror can neither silence nor drown.

Bernard of Clairvaux wrote of the eternal nature of conscience and Martin Luther said that 'Justice is a temporary thing that must at last come to an end; but the conscience is eternal and will never die.'

The Puritans, men soaked in Scripture, took the same view. Jim Packer says they 'spared no pains to impress upon men that they were working and playing in the ante-room of eternity' and believed that conscience 'continueth for ever in every man, whether he be in earth or heaven or hell'.

William Perkins, for example, extrapolates this from Romans 2:15–16, saying of conscience that it bears witness continually; not for a minute, or a day, or a month, or a year but forever. He says that

> when a man dies, conscience dieth not; when the body is rotting in the grave, conscience lives and is safe and sound: and when we shall rise again conscience shall come with us to the bar of God's judgement either to accuse or excuse us before God.

The Puritans went further than that. They held that 'both the happiness, and misery of Heaven and Hell, are from the inward frame of the conscience'. When speaking of the comfort of a good conscience, they often went on to make the point that it brings joy not only in life but also in death and at the judgement when the books are all opened, including the book of conscience. Like a man about to be married or someone who has paid off all their debts, so is a man with a good conscience at death. Those who lack such a thing will be filled with fear and the judgement day itself will be worse again. Ephraim Huit likens it to the case of Pharaoh's butler and baker and the negative and positive outcomes that befell them.

William Bates wrote that at the judgement each person's conscience will be opened and will condemn or approve him. 'There shall be an exact agreement' he suggests 'between the books of God's omniscience, and of conscience in the day of judgement'. Even the best consciences today are not entirely accurate. They can no more count all our sins than we can count the stars as they appear. However, he insists, 'one of the miracles of that day' will be what we today might call the data recovery that our consciences will engage in.

Conscience's judgements today anticipate to some extent the final judgement. This is why we must, in Sibbes' words, 'keep court at home first' and 'keep the assizes there' for by so doing we will have comfort in 'the great assizes' of heaven. Samuel Ward speaks of conscience not only as a 'petty heaven' here and, alluding to the death of Moses, a Mount Tabor 'glimpse of glory' but as the means of inconceivable joys in the world to come. He puts the company of a good conscience second only to the vision of God himself at that time and above the society of saints and angels. Like many others, he also believed conscience will be intolerable in hell and saw it as part of what makes hell the place it is.

Conscience in Heaven

In more recent years Robert Solomon has written of the sinless eternal state in heaven that 'the conscience will be a happy conscience' there, with nothing more to complain of.

Its only work will be to give a sense of well-being that we are in line with God's law, that all is well and that our relationship with God is intact. There will be no more guilty conscience.

William Ames declared that 'a *good conscience* ... is the *formal* and *essential* happiness of the Saints in the life to come.' To support his view he quoted Matthew 25:21 and its parallel in verse 23. These verses speak of the believer being commended at the last with a 'well done good and faithful servant'. John 15:11 and 1 Peter 1:8 speak similarly about seeing Christ in heaven and knowing complete joy.

That latter day Puritan C. H. Spurgeon once said that one of the 'best views we can ever give of heaven is, that it is a state of complete acceptance with God, recognised and felt in the conscience.' He says 'I suppose that a great part of the joy of the blessed saints consists in a knowledge that there is nothing in them to which God is hostile'.

The theme of conscience in heaven is perhaps otherwise underplayed by Puritan writers and their successors on the whole, although Richard Bernard does suggest that conscience will comfort us there because there will be nothing weak or sinful in us.

At that time, believers will be righteous and will be legally and not just evangelically obedient. Believers will find it not only possible not to sin, as is the case now, but it will not be possible to sin and so they will be perfectly sincere, loving and without hypocrisy. They will continue to have the presence of the Spirit and their fellowship with the Father and with the Son will be sweeter than ever. The conscience will witness to their being perfect in body and soul and it will convey to them the joy of that place. The heaven of heaven, we may say, will be the peace and joy of a good conscience.

Conscience in Hell

John MacArthur and John Blanchard have written in recent years of conscience in hell. MacArthur says 'No one's *conscience* will be silent then. It will turn on the sinner with a fury, reminding him that he alone is responsible for the agonies he will suffer eternally.' Blanchard says of the wicked that in hell *'their consciences will be their worst tormentors*. Nor will there be any way in which they can be stifled or silenced'.

Puritan writers have more to say about conscience in hell than conscience in heaven. Ames sees conscience as 'God's most powerful means to torment the reprobate'. In *The Saints everlasting rest* Baxter says

> Sinners shall lay all the blame on their own wills in hell forever. Hell is a rational torment by conscience, according to the nature of the rational subject. If sinners could but say, then, it was long of God, whose will did necessitate me, and not of me, it would quiet their consciences, and ease their torment, and make hell to be no hell to themselves. But to remember their wilfulness, will feed the fire, and cause the worm of conscience never to die.

The Puritans taught that conscience witnesses against the damned in hell and tortures them. Even though death itself cannot awaken conscience in some 'no sooner come they into hell, but conscience is there awakened to the full'. The conscience they thought hanged will then play the hangman.

Huit calls conscience one of the *Lord's executioners*, one of the vials of the wine of his indignation. He speaks of conscience in hell,

1. Upbraiding a sinner with his neglect and loss. He has neglected so many sound reproofs, sweet exhortations and gentle warnings and corrections. He has lost so many gracious promises, holy motions, redemption in Christ itself and the possibility of heavenly glory.

2. It wounds like a sword, gnaws like a worm and lashes like a whip in a man's heart. It may have slept in life but at that time it will shriek out loud.

3. It terrifies and scares—hence the weeping and howling that Jesus speaks so vividly of.

4. It 'subscribes the righteous judgement of the Lord' agreeing that the punishment is just. Its manner of working then will be rigorous, restless and eternal, however weak and fitful it may have been in life. One has only to see what conscience can do in this life to see that these things are so. Undoubtedly 'there will come a day when wicked men will approve religion, and wish a thousand times, that they had but one hour's respite'.

Many Puritans and others before them understood the never dying worm and the unquenchable fire to be referring to conscience. Dyke says that if the worm of hell should die, the fire would go out. That is to say, if the guilt of conscience could be removed then the punishment would end. Bernard connects the worm idea with being bred of corruption, 'gnawing and griping in the stomach and bowels' and constantly turning, each element pointing to evil conscience. Conscience drives home the sinner's ill desert to him in hell. As the worm never dies so the torment goes on—restless pain and an inability to die, with weeping and gnashing of teeth.

In the eighteenth century Jonathan Edwards, preaching on James 2:19, says of unbelievers, firstly

> When the King of heaven and earth comes to judgement, their consciences will be so perfectly enlightened and convinced by the all-searching light they shall then stand in, that their mouths will be effectually stopped, as to all excuses for themselves, all pleading of their own righteousness to excuse or justify them, and all objections against the justice of their Judge, that their conscience will condemn them only, and not God.

He also says that

> Natural conscience is not extinguished in the damned in hell; but, on the contrary, remains there in its greatest strength, and is brought to its most perfect exercise; most fully to do its proper office as God's vicegerent in the soul, to condemn those rebels against the King of heaven and earth, and manifest God's just wrath and

vengeance, and by that means to torment them, and be as a never-dying worm within them.

The Puritan Flavel argues that in hell the spirits of the damned become self-tormenters by means of the conscience. 'Conscience, which should have been the sinner's curb on Earth' he says 'becomes the whip that must lash his soul in hell.' No faculty or power in man is more suited to this task. 'That which was the seat and centre of all guilt, now becomes the seat and centre of all torments.' The suspension of its tormenting power in this world is a mystery. In this life the conscience can be remarkably quiet in some cases. But, he says,

> no sooner is the Christless Soul turned out of the body and cast for eternity at the bar of God but conscience is roused and put into a rage never to be appeased any more. It now racks and tortures the miserable soul with its utmost efficacy and activity. The mere presages and forebodings of wrath by the consciences of sinners in this world have made them lie with a ghastly paleness in their faces, a universal trembling in all their members, a cold sweating horror upon their panting bosoms, like men already in hell: but this, all this is but as the sweating or giving of the stones before the great rain falls. The activities of conscience (especially in Hell) are various, vigorous and dreadful to consider, such are its recognitions, accusations, condemnations, upbraidings, shamings and fearful expectations.'

He says six things about the conscience in hell.

1. The consciences of the damned will recognise and bring back to mind the sins committed in this world. He argues this on the basis that conscience is a register or Book of records that notes down every sin in its proper order. In Luke 16:25 Abraham says to the rich man 'Child, remember that you in your lifetime received your good things, and Lazarus in like manner bad things; but now he is comforted here, and you are in anguish.'

2. Conscience will charge and accuse the damned soul in hell and he will know that these charges and accusations are just and unanswerable.

3. Conscience will also condemn the sinner and with a dreadful sentence. It will support and approve of God's judgement. Every self-destroyer will be a self-condemner. 'This is a prime part of their misery'.

4. The upbraidings of conscience in hell are frightening and unsupportable.

> To be continually hit in the teeth and twitted with our madness, wilfulness and obstinacy as the cause of all that eternal misery which we have pulled down upon our own heads, what is it but the rubbing of the wound with salt and vinegar?

5. Further, the way conscience drives home guilt then will be an unbearable torment. We are ashamed of ourselves in this life when we are found out. In hell, a man's conscience throws his shame in

his face. There they are 'not only be derided by God but by their own consciences also'.

6. Conscience will also anticipate the further unending wrath to come in hell. Flavel sees this as 'the very sum and complement of their misery'. Just as a guilty man being held in prison is tortured by the thought of his coming trial and as a man on death row daily contemplates his fearful future so the souls of men in hell contemplate their unenviable future.

The weeping of damned sinners in hell is prompted by several considerations

Because they have lost heaven and its joys

Because they are suffering torment

Because they are with the devil and his angels and although they cry for mercy, no-one has pity on them.

They gnash their teeth in anger against themselves, the hellish spirits who enticed them in, one another, the godly who are now comforted, and against God, for they can neither repent nor will they give him glory.

The final words of Bernard's work on conscience are very solemn indeed. They are appropriate as the closing words to this brief chapter on conscience in the life to come and to the main body of this book. Do ponder them carefully.

Consider these woeful effects of this hell-worm hereafter, which now lieth at rest within thee, that hast hardened thy heart in wickedness. Oh betimes look to thy conscience, make it thy friend that God may be also thy friend, lest it become thy foe, and be the hell-worm among the damned fiends, there to torment thee for ever and for ever.

Appendix 1
A list of legitimate illustrations used to describe conscience and its workings

In writing of conscience and its workings Christians in different ages have sought to illustrate what conscience is by means of sometimes extended illustrations and metaphors. Here we list, with some explanations, some twenty-five of these. We could have added, perhaps, one more—the wheelbarrow, which, as Billy Graham once pointed out, illustrates how too many people follow their conscience—pushing it in the direction they want it to go! Otherwise here are 25 good illustrations'

1. Sundial. A sundial is an ancient means of telling the time of the day by the shadows cast by the sun. It is a useful tool provided the sun is shining. At night time or when it is overcast it is practically useless. The conscience also is very good at telling us what is right and wrong but only when the moral record is accurate. If that is corrupted or obscured then the conscience becomes practically useless.

2. Compass. A compass is a clock-like device that has a needle that always points to magnetic north. If you are lost but know in which direction north is you at least have some way of knowing where you are and how to get home. The properly functioning conscience is similarly able to show us in which direction to go. A compass can fail if a strong magnetic field other than the earth's own is present. Conscience can also be confused by false teaching. A compass can also fail to function properly if it is neglected and becomes rusty so that the needle does not point north as it should. Neglect of conscience can similarly lead to problems with its functioning.

3. Barometer. A barometer is a device that measures atmospheric pressure and so can give some idea of the approach of stormy weather. The conscience can likewise warn us beforehand of the possibility of falling into sin.

4. GPS system or Satnav. This increasingly common device relies on satellites in space to provide direction here on earth. At its best the information that conscience acts upon is heavenly wisdom as

revealed here on earth in Scripture. When this is accurate we can follow the dictates of conscience as confidently as we might a GPS.

5. Spy. The conscience can be likened to a spy, especially a sleeper, one who is in deep cover, as although the conscience is within a person there is a sense in which it is working for someone on the outside, for God himself and those who preach in his name.

6. Watchdog. Ideally a watchdog will bark at the approach of a stranger. Ideally, the conscience will protest when sin, to which we should be strangers, comes near.

7. Alarm bell. Like the watchdog illustration this emphasises the power of conscience to wake us up to danger from sin.

8. Wall or fence. A wall or fence sets the boundaries, the perimeter. Conscience does something similar when the moral record informs conscience proper of the contours that are to be followed.

9. Lash or whip. This illustration points to the pain conscience can sometimes inflict when it is active.

10. Sword. This is a similar picture showing again the wounds conscience can give when it is at work.

11. Bloodhound. A bloodhound is a hunting dog, one that can sniff out the quarry and then pursue it to the kill. A conscience

that has that sort of instinct with regard to sin is a good conscience indeed.

12. Window. This illustration simply reminds us that the conscience can give us an insight into our true moral state, provided the window is kept clean, as it were.

13. Mirror. This is a refinement of the window illustration stressing that when we look to conscience, what we see is essentially ourselves. Bernard uses it and the Puritan Fenner takes it up.

14. Sail. A sail, usually made of canvas, can be hoisted high and when it catches the wind the vessel is driven along. Conscience propels us along in the right direction when the Spirit of God informs it.

15. Plumbline or spirit level. Both are builder's tools. A plumbline is simply a piece of lead (plumb) attached to some string that when dropped reveals whether a wall is vertically true. The spirit level does the same for checking a horizontal true. Given that the conscience is meant to show us how we line up with what is right, these are good illustrations of its work.

16. Flight recorder or black box. Modern aeroplanes are fitted with flight recorders or black boxes (they are actually bright orange, to facilitate their being found after a crash). These are audio or data devices that record the conversation of the pilots and

information about controls and sensors, so that in the event of an accident investigators can investigate its causes. The conscience also keeps records that will one day be investigated as evidence.

17. Ear, nose or eye. Rehwinkel says 'Just as the ear is the sense organ for sound, the eye for light, the nose for smell, so conscience is the organ for ethical perception'.

18. Sense of taste. Our taste buds are found on our tongues and in our mouths. They enable us to detect the five (known) elements of taste perception: salty, sour, bitter, sweet and umami. It is conscience that gives us the ability to detect right and wrong in its various shades.

19. Courtroom. The Puritans loved to picture conscience as a court. The one accused is me. Conscience acts first as a witness against me then as a prosecutor or accuser. It is also a recorder or registrar writing it all down, as it were. Finally, it acts as judge and executioner, anticipating the final judgement to come.

20. Book or ledger. This biblical image occurs in several places such as Henry Burton's *Anatomy of melancholy*.

21. Diary. A diary is firstly compiled by recording events and then perused as a reminder. Conscience both records events and permits us to review them.

22. Guide. In London you sometimes see groups of tourists

being led by a guide holding an umbrella aloft or some other identifier. As long as the tourists keep their eye on the guide they will not be lost. And so if we let conscience be our guide we will know which way to go.

23. A bridle or brake. Some writers focus on the power of conscience to hold back from sin and so use the picture of a horse held back by a bridle or a brake on a car.

24. A mill. Henry Burton says that Egyptian hieroglyphs used this picture of grinding as the conscience works continually and its grinding is like torture.

25. Candle, torch or lamp. Because the conscience casts light on things, these are obvious illustrations of that power.

Appendix 2
The Argument for God from Conscience

Ezekiel Hopkins once wrote 'There is a conscience in man; therefore there is a God in heaven.'

There are several classic arguments for God's existence. One of these is what is sometimes called the moral argument. The conscience, it is said, proves the existence of a conscience giver. To put it another way, man's morality means that there must be a moral law giver.

Peter Kreeft notes that 'modern people often say they believe that there are no universally binding moral obligations, that we must all follow our own private conscience'. This very admission, he suggests, 'is enough of a premise to prove the existence of God'.

For all their subjectivism such people still hold that it is wrong to go against conscience. Even though consciences differ, there is still a moral absolute—'never disobey your own conscience'.

He then asks from where conscience gets such an absolute authority and suggests that there are only four possibilities.

1. From something less than me (nature)

2. From me (individual)

3. From others equal to me (society)

4. From something above me (God)

The argument is then that

1. I cannot be absolutely obligated by something less than me—animal instinct or practical need for material survival.

2. As I am not absolute I cannot obligate myself absolutely. Who am I to demand absolute obedience? I can obligate myself or decide that I am not obligated.

3. Society has no right to obligate me either, regardless of numbers. 'Society' is not God.

4. The only source of absolute moral obligation must be something superior to me binding 'my will, morally, with rightful demands for complete obedience.'

And so, it is argued, God, or something like God, is the only adequate source and ground for an absolute moral obligation to obey conscience. This leads Kreeft to insist, problematically we would say, that conscience 'is thus explainable only as the voice of God in the soul'.

Such proofs have a limited value but will perhaps help some to think about such matters and confirm those who already accept that God exists.

Appendix 3
A brief history of Christian thought with regard to the conscience and casuistry

Christians have long linked the study of conscience and *casuistry* (from the word *case*, Latin *casus*). Casuistry is 'the application of moral principles and the determination of right and wrong in particular cases in light of the peculiar circumstances and situation' (*New Dictionary of Theology*). The word has acquired negative and positive imports. Paul Helm called it 'an ugly word, with a chequered history ... synonymous with trickery, a falsification of the moral accounts' but concluded that 'we must all be casuists'!

Impartially, it seeks to give detailed moral guidance. More positively, it deals with proper moral action in single, concrete instances (*cases*). It is often spoken of in connection with special forms of discipline or to describe a branch of ethics. As it is impossible to frame express general moral rules for every situation, casuistry makes law more specific, less obscure and helps with application. It is an activity that goes back at least as far as the Pharisees.

Mention of the Pharisees, often condemned by Jesus, brings us back to the negative overtones. These arise when casuistry is used to provide excuses or permit unwarranted exceptions. Casuistry came into serious disrepute in the seventeenth century with the rise of certain Jesuits and an unprecedented organisation and documentation characterised in many people's eyes by moral laxity.

At the same time early Puritans such as Richard Greenham (1532–1591) and John Dod (1555–1645) were becoming famous for evangelical casuistry. According to Packer such people 'never wrote formal treatises of casuistry' but 'practised informally on friends and other troubled souls' and were 'famous for a season or two as powerful casuists'.

Before the Reformation

Early Development of Ideas of conscience and casuistry
Scattered references occur in early church fathers such as Origen (c 185–c 254), Tertullian (c 155–c 220) and Chrysostom (345–407). Douglas Milne says Augustine (354–430) 'worked on the idea of conscience as moral witness'. Later writers sometimes refer to the early writings. Early in sub-apostolic times a tendency is discernible to regulate moral life by outward legalism and foster a casuistic treatment of ethics. This disposition was further promoted in western theology under the influence of Stoic thinking. (The first book on casuistry was probably by the Stoic Cicero, 106–43 BC. 'We have each of us received from the immortal God a conscience which can by no means be separated from us'). There was also a tendency toward legalism in ecclesiastical doctrine, seen even in Augustine, that continued to be characteristic of the western catholic ethical system for many years.

There is some evidence to say that when Jerome (c 340–420) chose the Latin term *conscientia* to translate the Greek *syneidesis* he had a significant influence on subsequent generations. *Conscientia* for the Stoic, Michael Baylor says, meant 'man's awareness or lack of correspondence of his own actions to the law.' Stoic philosopher Seneca (4 BC–65 AD) used it to describe man's divine guardian within. Jerome further developed the idea writing on Ezekiel 1. Building on the Platonic three-fold division of man, he added a fourth, which 'the Greeks call *Synteresis*' that is the *scintilla conscientiae* or 'spark of the conscience which was not quenched even in the heart of Cain when driven from Paradise'. It is not entirely clear what he means by *synteresis* (it could be a copyist's misreading of *Syneidesis*). However, this term came to mark an important theological aspect of conscience. Muller's *Dictionary of Latin and Greek Theological Terms* says *synderesis* is a concept apparently from Aristotle, defined as 'the innate habit of the understanding which grasps basic principles of moral law apart from the activity of formal moral training'. (See too Muller's *Post-Reformation Reformed Dogmatics Vol. 1*). It is worth mentioning too that Peter Lombard (1100–1160) added to Jerome's Stoic influence with references to Seneca in his *Sentences*—'the great theological textbook of the Middle Ages'.

Ecclesiastical penance was the chief impetus to developing casuistry. This arose quite early and attracted to itself an elaborate ritual, including the imposition of ecclesiastical penalties for individual sins. The customary rules pertaining to the ancient forms of procedure and the relevant codified decrees of separate synods were collected, supplemented and arranged by compilers. Definitive manuals were made for confessors. Among the best known early ones are those attributed to Archbishop Theodore of Canterbury (d 690) and the Venerable Bede (d 735).

Medieval Theology

Further developments in casuistry were promoted by the entire method of scholastic ethics, with its subtle disputations; the influence of canonical repetition and the universally obligatory institution of auricular confession brought in at the Fourth Lateran Council, 1215. Such influences led to the rise of a distinctive systematic discipline, *theological* (as distinct from philosophic or legal) *casuistry*. A special class of teachers, casuists or schemists (distinct from canonists) cultivated it in the church and later the universities. Writings embodying the discipline are called *summa* (Latin for 'whole' or comprehensive) of cases of conscience.

Dominican Raymond Pennaforte (1175–1275) was author of one thirteenth century work. Many more appeared in the next two centuries, e.g. *Summae Astesana* (1317), *Pisana* or *Pisanella* (1338), *Pacifica* (c 1470), *Rosella, Angelica* (Luther once burned a copy in protest) and *Summa Summarum* or *Sylvestrinae* (1515). Antoninus of Florence (d 1459) is notable in this period as probably the first to treat moral theology as a distinct science, preparing the way for a closer union between moral theology and casuistry. Similar manuals followed, e.g. *Summala de Peccatis* by Thomas Cajetan (c 1469–1534).

As for *synteresis*, later work by Peter Abelard (1079–1142) and Franciscans Alexander of Hales (d 1245) and Bonaventura (1221–1274), says Baylor, led to the view that it is 'the ontological foundation of man's moral life' and a habit of the will. Seen as a collection of moral principles present in man's mind it was considered incapable of error and inextinguishable, unlike conscience, so fallible and subject to worldly influence. Conscience derives its authority from God. Any deviation from his will invalidates its moral authority.

Thomas Aquinas (c 1225–1274)

Dominican Albert Magnus (1206–1280), like his successors, saw *synteresis* as operating in the practical intellect, as it reasons to come to a decision about what to do in concrete situations. He amended this black-and-white view to include a wider scope for conscience's moral influence, introducing five levels of subjective certainty and holding that 'conscience binds where there is opinion, belief or certainty, but not merely doubt or ambivalence.' He was a big influence on Aquinas who, more than any other, was chief architect of the medieval understanding of conscience and a major influence on all subsequent theologians.

He saw *synteresis* as an infallible habit not a power. He assigned an unusual and unlikely etymology to *conscientia*, saying it was from *cum alio scientia*, 'knowledge applied to an individual case'. Essentially, conscience is an *act* of applying knowledge to particular cases. He also placed it in the practical intellect and spoke of a threefold activity—witnessing whether or not a thing was done; restraining from, encouraging to an act; passing judgement on.

The Reformers

By the Reformation period, penance had deteriorated into a form of commerce, leading Luther to declare (1519) 'there is nothing in the church that needs reform so much as confession and penance.'

He famously refused to recant in 1521 at Worms, saying, '… my conscience is captive to the Word of God, I cannot and I will not recant anything, for to go against conscience is neither right nor safe.' It was in the light of such struggles that he and others forged a renewed and biblically based understanding of conscience. The same year as his heroic stand, his *On Monastic Vows* defined conscience as not '... the power to do works, but to judge them.' He wrote, 'The proper work of conscience ... is to accuse or excuse ... Its purpose is not to do, but to pass judgement on what has been done, and this judgement makes us stand accused or saved in God's sight.'

Randall Zachman, writing on conscience in Luther and Calvin, observes Luther's distinction between conscience and the will, the will providing the conscience with its objects of judgement—that is, works. However, the object must arise from truth and a true conscience must arise from true teaching such that 'every doctrine creates a conscience.'

The 1530 *Augsburg Confession* deals with conscience in the chapters on repentance and good works, speaking of 'contrition, or terrors struck into the conscience' in repentance and how it is comforted and freed from terrors through faith; also of the comfort found in justification by 'godly and fearful consciences'. 'Consciences cannot be quieted by any works, but by faith alone'. Conflict is necessary first, then comes comfort. It comments that 'Formerly men's consciences were vexed with the doctrine of works; they did not hear any comfort out of the gospel. Whereupon conscience drove some into the desert, into monasteries, ... Others devised other works, whereby to merit grace, and to satisfy for sin. There was very great need, therefore, to teach and renew this doctrine of faith in Christ; to the end that fearful consciences might not want comfort, but might know that grace, and forgiveness of sins, and justification, are received by faith in Christ.'

According to Mark R. Shaw, writing on William Perkins, the author of the confession, Philip Melanchthon (1497–1560), developed the doctrine of conscience beyond Luther, and Calvin took things further again. Calvin rejected Roman casuists who had 'no more scruples than the Scribes and Pharisees about laying on men's shoulders burdens, which they would not touch with their finger' and who were intent on 'ensnaring men's souls' and seeking to 'tyrannously oppress consciences.' Like Luther and Melanchthon, however, he had a good deal more positive to say about conscience and the moral law.

Calvin defines conscience in terms of man's 'sense of divine judgement, as a witness joined to them, which does not allow them to hide their sins from being accused before the Judge's tribunal.' A good conscience is 'a certain mean between God and man, because it does not allow man to suppress within himself what he knows, but pursues him to the point of convicting him'. It is 'nothing but inward integrity of heart'. Its object is God and it binds 'without regard to other men.' Milne points out Calvin's stress on liberty of conscience, highlighting various elements in his treatment including the importance of the subject (of prime necessity); the fact the believer is free from the necessity of attaining righteousness through law (we are not to reckon what the law requires, but Christ alone, who surpasses all the perfection of the law, must be set forth as righteousness); how the believer conscientiously conforms himself to God's Law (delivered from the intolerable yoke of the Law he now submits himself to it with an obedience ready and joyful); also a freedom in regard to things indifferent (the knowledge of this freedom is very necessary for us, for if it is lacking, our consciences will have no repose and there will be no end to superstitions); he also deals with civil liberty. Though liberated in Christ from man's binding power, a Christian ought still to submit to the powers that be.

The Reformation introduced a multitude of new moral questions. In difficult situations people often appealed to the Reformers and their successors, or turned to university theology faculties. In this way Luther and Calvin's letters and Melanchthon's counsels furnished copious illustrations at large of evangelical resolutions of conscience. (E.g. Calvin to the Duchess of Ferrara on an oath imposed by her dying husband not to write to Calvin again! See, *Tracts and treatises on the Reformation of the church* Vol. 2). Systematic collections of faculty decisions mark the transition to an increasingly evangelical casuistry.

The Reformers also pointed in a new direction as regards the status of the individual conscience, one that ran wholly contrary to the Roman approach. As Carl Henry noted in *Christian Personal Ethics* 'The Roman Catholic conception that the church authoritatively mediated between God and man weakens the role of individual conscience. The individual is never permitted in that system to be directly confronted by the will of God in Scripture. The Jesuits urge that individual conscience be renounced for the authority of the church, on the alleged ground that the individual cannot now know what is right.'

This did not mean that each man was left to find his own way through the moral minefield. Ethics, it was seen, should be driven by a man's relationship with God and neighbour rather than 'loyalty to abstract principles rationally arrived at outside the context of the Christian community and its end' (Ian Breward introducing Perkins' works). Some have unfavourably contrasted Reformation ethics with what they see as a growing legalism in Protestant ethical thinking by the end of the sixteenth century. Karl Barth (1886–1968) cites Perkins' *De Cassibus Conscientae* as a notable example. This is part of a wider attempt to deny an organic connection between the Reformers and their successors. Paul Helm says that what the various arguments 'all come down to is ... Whereas Calvin's presentation ... was warm, exuberant and thoroughly evangelical, his ... followers presented what was introspective and legalistic. Sometimes it is held that the later Calvinists distorted ... Calvin ... other times the ... more serious claim is made, that the Puritans, supposedly followers of Calvin, were actually *opposed* to the teaching of Calvin in its central emphases.' Suffice to say that such views fail to do justice to the changed circumstances once the Reformation's initial insights had begun to permeate society.

Calvin's contribution to the doctrine of conscience, Milne insists, cannot be confined to his elucidation of Christian liberty. He agrees with Dowey that '... the term conscience is deeply embedded both in Calvin's utterly non-redemptive "natural" theology and in the very heart of his conception of justification by faith and of sanctification.' He speaks of 'the pervasive character of the notion of Conscience in his whole system of thought' not at 'the forefront of his dogmatics' but as a 'recurring motif'. In support, he instances the way his teaching is shaped by his understanding of conscience in three areas—anthropology (though fallen, man retains a consciousness of God, *sensus divinitatus*. Conscience is involved here—it does not allow us to sleep a perpetual sleep without being an inner witness and monitor of what we owe to God, without holding before us the difference between good and evil and thus accusing us when we fail in our duty.); soteriology (conscience works with the law to awaken men from their sin-induced stupor. This leads to despair of self and a desire to rest in Christ. Conscience can only be quietened—if unmerited righteousness be conferred upon us as a gift of God.); sanctification (a renewed conscience is a great asset in living a godly Christian life. A good conscience—is nothing but an inward uprightness of heart ... a lively longing to worship God and a sincere intent to live a godly and holy life. An innocent conscience strengthens a believer's faith and encourages him.)

Later Reformers wrote more directly on ethics. The French Calvinist Lambert Daneau (1530–1595) (*Ethices Christianae Libri Tres* 1577), spoke of a philosophical, scholastic or a preferred

Christian approach to ethics. Other writers include (see Keith Sprunger on Ames) German theologians Amandus Polanus (1561-1610) and Johannes Wollebius (1586-1629) as well as Perkins, Ames and, less directly, German Reformed theologian Bartholomäus Keckermann (1571-1609), Dutch Calvinist Antonius Walaeus (1573-1639), German Calvinist Encyclopaedist Johann Heinrich Alsted (1588-1638) (*Theologia Casuum* 1621, *Summa Casuum Conscientiae* 1628) and Wittenberg Lutheran Friedrich Balduin (1575-1627) (*Tractatus ... Casibus Nimirum Conscientiae,* 1628).

The Puritans

Medieval scholasticism influenced the Puritans and Reformers, especially Calvin. Puritanism was indeed a child of the Reformation, as Geoffrey Nuttall once put it. As far as developing the doctrine of conscience is concerned the Puritans built on their Reformation heritage, taking advantage of the relative calm after the storm to deal with difficulties that inevitably arose in the aftermath of Reformation. Milne says 'Far from being innovators' they 'were merely carrying forward emphases inherent in the Reformation movement itself. ... Calvin's doctrine constitutes an adumbration of the later Puritan teaching.'

It is suggested that the word *Puritan* came into fashion around 1556. Carl Trueman is not the first to observe how the word 'has proved notoriously difficult to define'. Writing on Owen, he says 'it remains true to say that it is easier to give examples of Puritans than give a precise and fully adequate definition of Puritanism'.

More analytically, Packer says that Puritan was an imprecise term of contemptuous abuse that was used for various groups between 1564 and 1642.

Historian Peter Lake says that 'the core of the moderate puritan position lay neither in the puritan critique of the liturgy and polity of the church nor in a formal doctrinal consensus' but 'in the capacity, which the godly claimed, of being able to recognise one another in the midst of a corrupt and unregenerate world'. They insisted on the 'transformative effect of the word on the attitudes and behaviour of all true believers.'

By *Puritans* we mean men of this sort, the group often identified with the 'spiritual brotherhood' of Greenham, Dod, Richard Rogers (1550–1620), Henry Smith (1550–1591), Arthur Hildersham (1563–1632) and their successors. To a man, they were convinced of the importance and centrality of plain, practical, expository preaching, emphasising conversion and godliness. It was chiefly concern for experiential religion that created their interest in conscience. The Reformers concern for church discipline also led to an inevitable focus on outward conduct and subsequent questions of conscience. Discussion of such matters in the Puritan *classis* (a proto-presbyterian meeting of ministers for discussion and policy agreement) such as the one that met at Dedham in the 1580s, was a catalyst for their thinking on casuistry. No doubt a further factor was a thirst for religious certainty and moral direction in changing times. It is this that prompted H. R. McAdoo to say (1949) that '... if a casuistry were not ready to hand, the atmosphere of seventeenth-century theology and politics would have made its invention imperative.'

Why did such interest not peak earlier? The new broom of the Reformation initially swept away much of the theory and practice characteristic of medieval pastoral care and at first had nothing to replace it. It soon became evident that Protestant practice did not live up to Protestant doctrine. 'Early optimism that faith and a good conscience would provide adequate guidance was soon replaced by a realisation that Christian liberty could be misunderstood.' Protestants became increasingly aware of differences between justification and sanctification, the importance of church and state discipline and the crucial role of the Ten Commandments in the Christian life and beyond. At the same time social and economic change and, from 1558, Elizabeth I's desire for a middle way that left the Church of England largely unreformed in structure, created a climate for change. In this period came the rise of Puritan casuistry.

Pastors found they needed to take time in their preaching to show the inseparability of faith and duty to society and spent significant amounts of time tackling pastoral problems that arose. For all their gifts, the Puritans were at first devoid of the well-honed pastoral routines characteristic of the best of the now resurgent Romanists. In 1603 Richard Rogers lamented how 'the Papists cast in our teeth that we have nothing set out for the certain and daily direction of the Christian'. Henry Holland (1583–1650?) complained that ministers tend rather to 'guess uncertainly to apply good remedies, than know how to proceed by any certain rules of art and well grounded practice.' Clearly many felt a new evangelical casuistry was needed, one that taught general principles rather than laying down rules. It was not likely to be forged overnight, however.

Jesuits

Scholastic Protestants such as the Puritans were willing to learn from their predecessors. Although the Reformation stands between the Puritans and Aquinas there is a measure of continuity. Examples of Puritan indebtedness to medieval theology are observable, for instance, in their practice of describing conscience as good, evil, erring, upright, etc. The beloved picture of the court of conscience, *forum conscientia*, is in Aquinas, Calvin and the Puritans. Ames is happy to use the work of Bishop Guillaume D'Auvergne (1105–1202). The Puritans 'were at once pioneers and traditionalists'. We should not be surprised either at their placing conscience in the practical understanding in line with Aquinas or their rejecting his idea that the *synteresis* has some sort of infallibility.

While happy to learn from the past, with the more recent Roman casuists there was ambivalence. While willing to learn from anyone, casuistry had become 'well nigh inseparable from the confessional', making for obvious difficulties. The Puritans were concerned not to provide manuals for confessors but instructions 'for all reasonable and devout Christians ... worthy to be followed with all care by all men.' By their diligence they were able to make the seventeenth century one in which, uniquely, casuistical divinity became a subject of popular interest. Further, Protestants, and some Catholics too, were wary of the 'mischievous science' of the Jesuits. For example, their doctrine of probabilism, which taught that in doubtful cases, one may follow any probable opinion however remote, was wide open to abuse. They also encouraged equivocation and over-subtle distinctions between means and ends. Within Papistry, rigorists (chiefly Jansenists) and laxists (chiefly Jesuits) fell to disputing. Dominican Baptiste Gonet (1616–1681) condemned such quibbling with God, and Blaise Pascal (1623–1662) in his 1656 Provincial Letters famously attacked Jesuit casuistry. Hailed a satirical classic, it was a body blow from which the Jesuits never recovered. Pascal remained a Romanist but Protestants loved his work. (Within Romanism, casuistry was later refined by e.g. Lambertini, *Casus conscientiae*, 1763; Sobiech *Compendium theologiæ moralis*, 1822).

Ames' speaks of 'some veins of silver' in the midst of 'a great deal of earth and dirt' out of which he drew 'some things that are not to be despised' but warns against 'death in the pot'. His desire is that the children of Israel will not need to go down to the Philistines (Papists) to have their tools sharpened in the future. Even as late as the time of Baxter the same concerns were being expressed.

William Perkins 1558–1602

Two figures stand out among Puritan writers on conscience. These are William Perkins and William Ames. With Baxter, Gordon Wakefield says they were 'the most outstanding and exhaustive of the Puritans' in seeking to resolve cases of conscience. Perkins was 'perhaps the most significant English theologian of his age', 'prince of puritan theologians ... most eagerly read', 'mightiest preacher' and 'most widely known theologian of the Elizabethan church', one who made a 'quite extraordinary contribution' in the area of casuistry and conscience.

Warwickshire born, of godly parents, he was converted from an apparently decadent life at Christ's College, Cambridge, becoming a faithful preacher and a prolific author. He had tremendous repute as a pastor and a good deal of experience gleaned from hours spent resolving 'cases of conscience'. His *A resolution to the Countriman* gives a foretaste of his desire to resolve such cases. It is his major works on the subject, however, that earn him the title 'a master Protestant casuist' and in moral casuistry 'the first great master of the form' (McKim, Muller).

These works include *A discourse of conscience: wherein is set down the nature, properties and differences thereof as also the way to get and keep a good conscience* (1596). Three other books emerged, which Perkins was working to synthesise at the time of his death. These appeared posthumously, in 1606, as *The whole treatise of the cases of conscience distinguished into three Bookes*. Only the first part was revised and corrected by Perkins. In 1592 it had been one of the first books where 'Reformed theology took precedence in the elaboration of casuistry'. A second part was first published in 1595; the third was appearing for the first time.

Other Puritans refer to conscience and see its importance but 'Perkins represents a new phase in the progressive development of Reformed teaching'. His work 'was truly historic since he initiated not only a Puritan but a Protestant casuistry' (Milne). Markham calls his 'understanding of conscience ... the central factor in his writings'. His unique approach provided 'a fresh outlook on the problems plaguing the lives of his fellow men'. Shaw similarly claims that 'the key to Perkins' thought is found in his casuistry ... a torch to re-ignite the existential dynamic of the faith so visible in the thought and experience of' the Reformers. Perkins showed, in L. John Van Til's words, 'an intense interest in conscience not found in the works of his puritan peers.' Van Til argues that it is not going too far to say that he introduced a whole 'theology of conscience'. It is not that he cast aside previous Puritan distinctives but that he sought to view them all through the prism of conscience, identifying it as the key to enabling the Christian to accurately keep his soul in the state it should be.

William Ames 1576-1633

The other great Puritan writer on conscience is Ames, a one-time pupil of Perkins. Ralph Bronkema calls him '... the greatest theologian that Puritanism produced'. A hotter sort of Protestant, his strong Puritan views forced him to join others of like mind on the continent where he became Theology Professor in Franeker, Friesland, producing two major works—The *Medulla Theologica* (1623, enlarged 1627, later published as *The Marrow of Sacred Divinity*) and a companion volume on conscience, based on his doctoral work (1630) *De Conscientia*. This work focuses first on the workings of conscience then systematically treats the Commandments, giving specific applications for daily Christian living. Thus it engages in biblical casuistry. He 'imparted a new fullness and scope to the field explored by Perkins' (Milne). To say, as Van Til says that 'the similarity between what Perkins and Ames had to say about conscience all but ended with the word *conscience*' is a distortion but there are significant differences.

Sprunger identifies three chief elements in Ames—Ramist philosophy, orthodox Calvinist theology and Puritan moral piety, qualities also found in Perkins and, to a degree, other Puritans. Contrary to Sprunger, Milne says that the Ramist influence was nothing more than the employment of a useful methodology. Sprunger also says that Ames 'always emphasised biblical exegesis and practical theology' always balancing 'doctrine and the practical application.' The pattern goes back to Paul, of course, but Muller sees Ames as following a Puritan methodological pattern in publishing not only a major work on theology but also a major practical treatise and suggests a similar phenomenon is observable in Perkins who developed 'not only a system of casuistry but also a system of doctrine, which he developed at considerable length in *An exposition of the Creede.*'

The *Marrow* itself exhibits this pattern, notably beginning 'Theology is the doctrine of living to God' and proceeding to divide between faith, the doctrines, and observance, the practical, moral application. He says 'Every precept of universal truth pertaining to living well in either economics, politics, or law very properly belongs to theology'. Sprunger quotes Increase Mather (1639-1723) commending Ames, 'It is rare for a scholastical wit to be joined with an heart warm in religion, but in him it was so'. Not all Protestant theologians were then taking this approach.

Middle period Puritans

Perkins and Ames easily dominate but are not alone. A number of writers wrote on conscience in this period. University men, mostly Cambridge, often college fellows, all were preachers, sometimes with other roles. They often suffered to a degree for nonconformity. What links them is a desire not simply to see God's Word preached but lived out by those who submit their consciences to what is preached.

In 1617 the first sermon at popular open air pulpit, Paul's Cross, by Samuel Ward (1577-1634) *Balm from Gilead to Recover Conscience* (on Hebrews 13:18) was published. It was often reprinted. Well known Puritan Richard Sibbes (1577-1635) published little in his life-time but after his death friends began to publish his works. He refers to conscience in various places, especially his exposition of 2 Corinthians 1 where he deals at length with verse 12.

More obscure are Jeremiah Dyke (1584-1639) and Ephraim Huit (c1608-1644). Dyke's long preaching career was supplemented by a number of publications on practical divinity, including his most successful, *Good Conscience* (Acts 23:1-3). It ran to six editions, 1623-1635. Huit's *The anatomy of conscience or the Summe of Paul's*

Appendix 3: A brief history of Christian thought 235

regeneracy (Acts 24:16), appeared in 1626. Richard L. Greaves says of Richard Bernard (1568–1641) 'pastoral experience was the basis for *Christian See to thy Conscience* (1631), which offered remedies for consciences that were blind, superstitious ... or otherwise ailing.' Westminster Divine Robert Harris (1578–1658) saw two bulky volumes of sermons published in 1654. One contains eight sermons on conscience originally published in two volumes (1630). In a preface to *The Souls Looking Glasse* (1643) by William Fenner (1600–1640), his successor in his lengthiest pastorate, Edmund Calamy (1600–1666) wrote that while there were a great 'many good books written, ... there wanteth one book to make us put those good books into practice ... this book ... may have this happy effect'. Chiefly on conscience, the text is Romans 2:15. Other works include three very brief ones by Greenham (1595), one by Walker the Ironmonger (*fl* 1638–1660) 1641, Thomas Riley's *Triall of Conscience* (1639). Also see parts of John Sedgwick (c 1600–1643) *The bearing of the burden by the spirit* (Proverbs 18:14).

A number of Puritan titles in this period use the word *conscience*. For example, Thomas Sparke 1548–1616, *A Short Treatise Very Comfortable For All Those Christians That Be Troubled and Disquieted in Theyr Consciences* (1580); Richard Kilby d 1617, *The Burthen of a Loaden Conscience* (1608); Robert Bolton *A Treatise On Comforting Afflicted Consciences* (1626).

Later Puritans

The flow of sermons and books on conscience from Puritan writers did not dry up with the coming of the Westminster

Assembly. The Confession itself makes several references to conscience, notably 20.2 'God alone is Lord of the conscience, and has left it free from the doctrines and commandments of men that are in any thing contrary to his Word, or beside it in matters of faith or worship. So that to believe such doctrines, or to obey such commandments out of conscience, is to betray true liberty of conscience; and the requiring an implicit faith, and an absolute and blind obedience, is to destroy liberty of conscience, and reason also. (See also 17.3 the consciences of believers being wounded and hurt; 18.1 assurance for those who truly believe in the Lord Jesus, and love him in sincerity, endeavouring to walk in all good conscience before him; 18.4 things that diminish assurance and wound conscience. Also conscience of duty as one of the means to regaining assurance; 22.6 conscience of duty again, among other things, in taking an oath; 23.4 honouring the powers that be for conscience's sake.)

Just as Puritanism continued in some measure at least to the end of the seventeenth century, so did books on conscience. In 1642 *The Booke of Conscience Opened and Read* (Proverbs 15:15) by John Jackson (c 1621-1693) appeared. Also note John Sheffeild (sic) (d 1680?) *A Good Conscience the Strongest Hold* (1650); William Twisse (1578?-1646) *The Doubting Conscience Resolved* (1652); Daniel Cawdrey (1588-1664) a brief exposition of 1 Timothy 1:9 (1655).

Other writers on the subject include Samuel Rutherford (1600-1661) *A Free Disputation Against Pretended Liberty of Conscience*

(1649) which concerns the church and state question. There was some controversy over this and the debate between Roger Williams and John Cotton in New England was very significant, while the unfolding history of England between 1662 and 1689 was full of interest. Decent surveys on the long history of church state relations are found in J. Marcellus Kik *Church and State, the story of two kingdoms* (1963) and, more recently, Chapter 3 of Don Carson's *The Intolerance of Tolerance*. Chapter 6 of Rutherford's *Ane Catachism Conteining the Soume of Christian Religion* is full of interest being chiefly on conscience in general.

Samuel Clark (1599–1682) produced several works in this area (*Golden Apples* 1659 *Of Scandal* 1680, etc.). David Dickson wrote on cases of conscience in *Therapeutica Sacra* (Latin 1656, English 1664, etc). James Durham (1622–1658), co-author with Dickson of the influential *Summe of saving knowledge*, also wrote on conscience in *Heaven upon earth* (1685) and on cases of conscience in *The Law unsealed* (1675) a practical exposition of the Commandments.

The Morning Exercise at Cripplegate or Several Cases of Conscience practically resolved by sundry ministers, some 75 in all, appeared also in 1660, under the editorship of (aptly named) Thomas Case (1598–1682) and subsequently in 1661 and 1664, edited by Samuel Annesley (1620?–1696) who wrote often on cases of conscience. Joseph Alleine (1634–1688) produced *Divers Practical Cases of Conscience Satisfactorily Resolved* (1672) and the following year his brother-in-law John Norman (1622–1669) added *Cases* of Conscience Practically Resolved. Richard Alleine (1611-1691), Joseph's father-in-law, wrote *Instructions about heartwork* with a section on conscience. In 1676 Nathanael Vincent (1639?-1697) published on conscience *A heaven or hell upon earth*. Henry Stubbes (1606?-1678) published *Conscience the best friend upon earth* (1673).

Among the works of Bishop Ezekiel Hopkins (1633-1690) is his brief *On the nature, corruption and renewing of the conscience* (Acts 24:16). There are also insights into conscience in published works by Puritan giants such as Thomas Goodwin, Thomas Brooks (1608-1680), John Owen (1616-1668), Thomas Manton and Stephen Charnock (1628-1680). Bunyan's Mr Conscience in his *Holy War* reveals a Puritan understanding. In 1653 Baxter published *The right method for a settled peace of conscience*. He followed this 20 years later with his massive and comprehensive *Christian Directory*, a 'sum of practical theology and cases of conscience'. It has been called 'a lasting monument to Puritan endeavour in this field' and includes discussions of the conscience and much more. It is so exhaustive, it is unsurprising that nothing on such a scale was attempted again.

Later works, not necessarily Puritan, include Henry Hammond *Of Conscience* 1645; Thomas Fuller *Cause and cure of a wounded conscience* 1647; Joseph Hall *Resolutions and decisions of divers practical cases of conscience, etc.* 1650; Robert Sanderson, various works; Alexander Ross *Picture of a Christian man's conscience* 1648;

Jeremy Taylor *Ductor Dubitantium or Rule of conscience* 1660; John Sharp *A discourse of conscience/Case of a doubting Conscience* 1685.

After the Puritans

After the Puritan era Protestant interest in conscience and casuistry seems largely to have faded. Jonathan Edwards (1703–1758) gives a chapter to conscience in his *The nature of virtue* and in 1755 Pike and Hayward published their two volume *Some important Cases of Conscience* but these are rare exceptions to the general rule.

Meanwhile, philosophers such as Immanuel Kant (1724–1804) began to think in entirely naturalistic ways. 'For Kant' writes Ash 'conscience becomes a merely subjective and individual guide'. By the time of Gilbert Ryle (1900–1976) and his seminal essay *Conscience and moral convictions*, conscience is seen as not relating nor able to relate to any wider authority. The idea of an outside authority dictating what a person is to believe is considered absurd.

Another significant influence on modern understanding of conscience is the work of Sigmund Freud (1856–1939) who famously wrote of the id, ego and super-ego in man. 'The long period of childhood, during which the growing human being lives in dependence on his parents, leaves behind it as a precipitate the formation in his ego of a special agency in which this parental influence is prolonged. It has received the name of super-ego. In so far as this super-ego is differentiated from the ego or is opposed to it, it constitutes a third power which the ego must take into account.' Freud equated the super-ego pretty much with conscience. For him all that is found in the moral record is merely cultural and never entirely reliable. Bad feelings are only feelings, not genuine guilt. Conscience is merely cultural baggage that I do well to break free from.

Rehwinkel gives a chapter to interacting with naturalistic writers. He concludes, 'they make bold assertions and sweeping claims for their theories and clothe them in mysterious verbiage and impressive technical jargon, but they do not prove their claims'. His chief argument is that whereas they assert that conscience is 'the result of accumulated experiences of utility, gradually organised and passed on by heredity' they cannot explain the gap between utility and morality or the origin of religion. Given that conscience often upbraids us, how can we explain it as a survival instinct or some other product of evolution? Where does the worship instinct come from?

Relatively little has been done by evangelicals to counteract this post-enlightenment rejection of biblical views. There has been a very slow but steady trickle of titles in this century and the last, seeking to uphold biblical views, including the pioneering book by the Dane, Ole Hallesby that first appeared in 1933. There have also been slim popular works by Rehwinkel (1956), Jerry White (1979), Wiersbe (1983), Peter Toon (1984), Zodhiates (1985), MacArthur (1994) and most recently Robert Solomon (2010) and Christopher Ash (2012).

A Select Bibliography

Puritan works
William Perkins, *Whole treatise of the cases of conscience*, 1608
Richard Bernard, *Christian see to thy conscience*, 1630
William Ames, *Consciences with the power and cases thereof*, 1639
William Fenner, *The soul's looking glass*, 1640
James Durham, *Heaven upon earth*, 1685
Richard Sibbes, *Complete Works*, Vol. 3, Nichol, Edinburgh, 1862

Later works
John King, *Conscience considered chiefly in reference to moral and religious obligation*, Seeley and Burnside, London, 1838
O Hallesby, *Conscience*, IVP, London, 1933
C. A. Pierce, *Conscience in the New Testament*, SCM, London, 1955
Alfred Rehwinkel, *The voice of conscience*, Concordia, St Louis, 1956
J Marcellus Kik, *Church and State*, Nelson, New York, 1963
John Van Til, *Liberty of Conscience*, Craig Press, Nutley NJ, 1972
David Fountain, *Let Conscience Speak*, Henry Walter, Worthing, 1973

Warren Wiersbe, *Meet your conscience*, Back to the Bible, 1983
Peter Toon, *Your conscience as your guide*, Church Publishing, 1984
John MacArthur, *The vanishing conscience*, Word, Dallas, 1994
Robert Solomon, *The Conscience*, Armour, Singapore, 2010
Christopher Ash, *Pure joy*, IVP, Leicester, 2012